THE VOLUNTARY CHURCH

THE
VOLUNTARY
CHURCH

American Religious Life (1740-1865)
Seen Through the Eyes of
European Visitors

MILTON POWELL, *Editor*

THE MACMILLAN COMPANY · NEW YORK
COLLIER-MACMILLAN LTD · LONDON

Permission to reprint from the following material is gratefully acknowledged:

Prince Napoleon in America, 1861, by Camille Ferri Pisani and translated by Georges J. Joyaux, Indiana University Press, 1959

America: A Sketch of Its Political, Social and Religious Character, by Philip Schaff and edited by Perry Miller, The Belknap Press of Harvard University Press, Copyright, 1961, by the President and Fellows of Harvard College

Gentleman's Progress: The Itinerarium of Dr. Alexander Hamilton edited by Carl Bridenbaugh, The University of North Carolina Press and the Institute of Early American History and Culture

Library of Congress Catalog Card Number: 67–19678

FIRST PRINTING

The Macmillan Company, New York

Collier-Macmillan Canada Ltd., Toronto, Ontario

Printed in the United States of America

For Sue,
my collaborator on a previous and
current anthology

CONTENTS

PREFACE

THE PREDOMINANT FORM of religious organization in Western civilization has been the state church. In America, nearly two centuries ago, an alternative pattern began to emerge, characterized by freedom of conscience, constitutional separation of church and state, and voluntary support of religious activity. The "voluntary church" has prevailed in America, and many of its features have been adopted by European nations as well. Yet at one time it was something very new under the sun and was a feature of American life that attracted much attention from foreign observers. From among the hundreds of travel accounts that deal with American religion in some way, I have selected those which comment most meaningfully upon the voluntary system during the period in which it developed into its present form.

Most of the expenses encountered in preparing this volume were met by two research grants from Michigan State University. Dr. Franklin Littell gave valuable encouragement and advice at an early stage in the project.

East Lansing, Michigan
Christmas, 1966

INTRODUCTION

AT THE VERY CLOSE of F. Scott Fitzgerald's novel *The Great Gatsby* the narrator, Nick Carraway, walks down to the beach of Gatsby's Long Island estate. The houses seem to disappear in the dusk while the land, water, and trees remain visible. For a moment Nick experiences what the first Dutch sailors must have felt when they approached "a fresh, green breast of the new world," that confrontation when man came "face to face for the last time in history with something commensurate to his capacity for wonder."

It requires Fitzgerald's powers to recapture that sense of wondrous curiosity which America aroused in the European imagination only a few centuries ago. Europeans are no longer curious about us, nor, for that matter, are we curious about them. The communications revolution has obliterated the ignorance in which the curiosity was grounded—though it has not replaced it with understanding. If a European visitor writes a book now about America, he does so not for Europeans but for Americans. For there has been no obliteration of our curiosity about ourselves, of our desire to see ourselves as others see us. This curiosity of Americans about America has kept us attentive to the observations of European travelers from the time of Crèvecoeur and de Tocqueville to that of Gunnar Myrdal and Denis Brogan. And we have profited from the attention. Not only have we learned much from European visitors, but our evaluation of the American experience has been strongly influenced by them. The combination of cultural kinship and relative detachment in the mind of a sensitive, sharp-eyed European has frequently provided a perspective upon our behavior which cannot be matched by the indigenous student.

This, then, is the first premise of this book: that we can learn and have learned much that is important about ourselves from studying the reactions of thoughtful Europeans to their experience of American life. The second premise is that although the organization of religion was one of the most striking features of American society in the eighteenth and nineteenth centuries, students of religion in America have not fully utilized the wealth of pertinent comment and criticism on this topic that exists in the accounts of European travelers.

Reflective Europeans who visited America in the eighteenth and nineteenth centuries were preoccupied with the phenomenon of European institutions developing under different geographic and political conditions. But beyond this they were curious about the progress and prosperity of indigenous American experiments. Certainly the secular experiments with republican institutions and political democracy were of paramount importance. But Europeans were also aware that the voluntary church,[1] the result of religious diversity in the colonial period and the constitutional separation of church and state, was a phenomenon unique in the history of Christendom.

For fifteen centuries the standard pattern of ecclesiastical organization had been the state church, in Catholic and Protestant nations alike. Though some nations, such as England, had taken steps in the direction of toleration, these measures still presupposed the existence of a privileged establishment. Religious freedom and voluntary church support were considered as radical in the minds of most Europeans as were the principles of democracy.

It was with a great deal of interest therefore, that Europeans observed the development of this unique arrangement through its successive stages: the explicit provisions for religious freedom in Rhode Island, Pennsylvania, and Maryland, the enforced acquiescence in religious diversity of the colonial establishments, the disintegrating effects of the Great Awakening, and finally the emergence, under the impact of rationalism and political independence, of a pluralistic, disestablished, voluntary system of religious organization.

European travel literature has been used with great effectiveness by students of America's secular institutions. It is with the intention of bringing similar accounts to bear upon the development of our unique religious institutions that I have gathered together in this volume the pertinent comments of European observers on those institutions during the formative period of their history, 1740–1865.[2]

Like all travel literature, the accounts of American religious phenomena given by European travelers vary widely in quality and perspective. Many are concerned only with the eccentricities of particular denominations and sects. For the purposes of this volume therefore, I have limited the selections to those which deal most explicitly with the development and nature of the voluntary system as a whole. The variety of perspectives is another matter. While somewhat confusing at first glance, it will, I trust, prove to be a rich source of insights into the peculiar nature of our religious institutions and behavior.

Many Europeans came to America with rather firm predispositions and expectations, and their accounts of American religious life are (like some accounts of our political institutions) correspondingly biased. Rationalists, for example, came expecting to find Christianity withering away as a result of the loss of its privileged position within the state. Proponents of European establishments arrived full of dire predictions about the chaotic effects of religious diversity upon American society. Roman Catholics expected to see a rampant Protestantism displaying its worst aspects and were curious about the prosperity of their faith under conditions of religious freedom and voluntary support. Dissenters from European establishments, somewhat in the manner of democrats and radicals, hoped to find that the success of the American experiment would provide a basis for its eventual adoption on their side of the Atlantic.

Within this diversity it is possible to discern a number of recurring questions which Europeans raised about religion in America. They were concerned first of all with the relationship between voluntaryism and the religious habits of Americans. Did

Americans seem to be more or less pious than Europeans? To what extent did their religious associations affect their private lives? What were the characteristic manifestations of religious sentiment on public occasions? What were the peculiar styles of preaching in the free American pulpits, and what responses to them were typical? What could one say about the effect of religious freedom upon America's morals?

Europeans were also interested in the prosperity of religious institutions under a set of circumstances which had no precedent in their experience. What would be the fate of churches which were entirely dependent upon voluntary support? How would churches be built, salaries paid? What powers would ministers have who were dependent upon the congregation they served for financial support? What concept of the church would emerge from this conglomeration of voluntary associations? Would not the inherent schismatic tendencies of Protestantism reach, under these conditions, their logical end in the division of American Christianity into an infinite number of jealous and autonomous sects? Or might the opposite happen, and the Americans, free now from secular, national loyalties, be able to find the key to religious unity on a purely spiritual basis? Implicit in all of these questions was that of the extent to which European Christianity had suffered or benefited from its own development under artificial conditions of state patronage.

Europeans were further interested in the relationship between voluntaryism and America's political institutions. Could a stable society exist without an establishment? If, as Montesquieu claimed, a republic must be founded upon the virtue of its citizens, and if, as most Europeans and Americans believed, virtue must have a religious foundation, could a nation safely afford to leave its churches dependent upon voluntary popular support? Or if, as radicals and rationalists insisted, civic virtue consisted solely in the application of reason to public affairs, were not the Americans making a serious error by allowing ministers and priests to proselyte without restriction and supervision, and to extend the influence of their effete supernaturalism? But perhaps religious freedom was a shrewd application of the ideas of the French *politique*, a policy which would result in religion becoming a private, compartmentalized concern, leaving the citizen free to conduct his civic affairs on an entirely secular basis. Then what was to be the public role of the minister under such circumstances? Did the separation of church and state necessarily preclude some kind of theocracy? Would it not be possible for American religious leaders to achieve great power through their influence over their congregations and within their denominations? How did the clergy envision their role in American political life? To what extent did they consider it appropriate to deal with matters of public policy in their pulpits? How did they distinguish between their roles as ministers and as citizens? And again, what about religious diversity and sectarian rivalry? Regardless of its impact upon the churches, what would it be upon the state? Would denominational jealousy prove to be a disintegrative force in American life? Could the American republics retain political unity despite religious disunity? Could the American people achieve any national loyalty without a national church?

Finally, Europeans were curious about the future of the voluntary church itself. Would this unique arrangement prove to be successful and thereby become a permanent feature of American society? Would one denomination, more aggressive or more persuasive than its competitors, be able to achieve a privileged position and restore the European system in some formal or informal manner? Or would a coalition of denominations emerge, a "Church of America," powerful enough to bring about its establishment? Perhaps, as some rationalists hoped, religion itself would disappear, the natural result of the withdrawal of that artificial sanction which had been, presumably, the sole cause of its continued existence in Europe.

Students of American social, intellectual, and institutional history will find much that is useful to them in these excerpts. As Alexis de Tocqueville first pointed out, America's development as a nation has taken place in the absence of feudal institutions. Consequently, the basic principle of all our social organization is that of voluntary association. We are, as we are so often told, a nation of joiners and, of course, of resigners as well. Thoreau's classic objection was directed toward an exception to the rule; ordinarily Americans are not considered to be members of corporations they have not joined. The history of American religion therefore is the history of the application of the principle of voluntary association to the religious life of the American people, and as such, it serves as a useful case study of the principle itself. Moreover, the voluntary church has had a profound influence upon American cultural and intellectual history. Religion has had a crucial role in the formation of public opinion, and this role cannot be properly assessed unless the nature of voluntaryism itself is thoroughly understood. It is a commonplace observation that in America moral issues become political issues and political issues become moral issues. The views contained in this book will, I trust, throw some light upon the circumstances which have made this so.

Church historians and students of religion in American life will find this a valuable collection of sources and supplementary readings. For the latter these excerpts will provide that sense of personal experience which has always been a major contribution of travel literature to the study of the past. For the former they will reinforce a tendency in the study of American church history to focus attention upon the voluntary church itself as the adaptation of European Christianity to the social and institutional environment of America, an environment in which the basis of ecclesiastical polity is the principle of voluntary association in circumstances of religious and ethnic diversity and in the absence of a religious establishment. It was certainly this feature of American religious life that attracted the most comment from foreign observers.

These accounts will also have much relevance for those ministers and laymen who are concerned with the shape and function of the church in contemporary American life. It is no exaggeration to say that the Christian churches in this nation are experiencing a period of such extensive reappraisal that one must turn to the sixteenth century to find comparisons. To be fruitful this re-examination must be grounded in a thorough understanding of the voluntary system and its historical development, for the institutional shape of American churches and their modes of operation have been formed by this historic experiment. This is not the place for a comprehensive survey of the issues which fill the pages of denominational journals these days, but it is appropriate to suggest the contribution these excerpts can make to the discussion.

Contemporary churchmen are concerned, for example, with the organic shape of the church. The basic unit of church organization in America is the self-sustaining congregation. In the search for alternatives to this form which will serve the varied needs of a complex industrial, urban society, it is of crucial importance that the self-sustaining congregation itself be understood as a direct result of voluntaryism.

In the absence of an establishment, local congregations were forced not only to become financially self-supporting units but to find some means of achieving legal standing in a secular society. As Murat pointed out,[3] they took on the nature of corporations and were thus able to hold property and, as legal persons, to enjoy equal protection of the laws. The congregational structure remains closely related to the legal status of a corporation, and attempts to modify it or to construct alternatives to it must include an awareness of the relevant implications. Just what is the legal status of a body of worshipers which is not financially self-sustaining—*i.e.*, of the "mission church"?

A very closely related problem is that of the church's role in movements for social reform. The American churches can affect public policy only by their powers of persuasion. Yet at the same time they are dependent upon voluntary support for their continued existence as institutions. The minister who champions an unpopular cause runs the risk of bringing economic disaster upon his congregation by the departure from it of those who are alienated by his views. The same dilemma exists at successive levels of any denominational hierarchy. One solution, common in the early nineteenth century, was to organize efforts for social reform into separate voluntary associations—temperance and abolition societies, for example—encouraged by, but not officially identified with the denomination. In this way, those who were moved to work for social reform could do so under religious auspices, while those who opposed it did not necessarily feel disposed to withdraw their support from the denomination on that account. Today the major denominations face the dilemma of either withdrawing from active official participation in social reform or suffering the loss of members and funds if they do not. Probably, though less apparently, they will suffer in either case. Here again a full understanding of the risks and opportunities requires a better understanding of the nature and history of the voluntary church than most denominational leaders now possess.

All these considerations lead me finally to what ought to be called a thesis—if an anthology can have a thesis. We have assumed that the voluntary church has worked almost perfectly in America, that the genius of its conception has been confirmed by its practical success. In recent years, however, sociological analyses by H. R. Niebuhr, Will Herberg, Peter Berger, Gerhard Lenski, and others have revealed serious weaknesses and limitations. We have learned that denominationalism may reflect the capitulation of religion to national, racial, and economic differences; that religion is exploited as a means of identifying oneself as an American; that Americans are largely ignorant of the content of their faith; that religious belief does not figure prominently in decision making; and that the churches are apparently unable to lead popular opinion on important social issues. The most frequent explanation of these phenomena is that they are of recent origin—the twentieth century or the immediate post-Civil War era at the earliest. However, the anticipation of these findings by some of the most perceptive foreign observers (e.g., Godley, Grund, Murat) suggests that their origins are to be found in the period of the late eighteenth and early nineteenth century and their causes in the structure and function of the voluntary church.

NOTES

[1] I have used the term "voluntary church" to denote the unique pattern of religious organization which emerged in American society during the period covered by this book. The chief features of the voluntary church are the constitutional restriction of an establishment, the absence of an official creed and religious tests, and the consequent reliance of all religious institutions upon voluntary support. This term is roughly synonymous with "denominationalism," which most recent scholars have employed for the same phenomena, but is more useful as a descriptive term, since it lacks the pejorative connotations which "denominationalism" has always carried. In addition, it is more closely related to terms which were actually employed during the period, such as "voluntaryism," "voluntary system," and "voluntary principle."

[2] 1740, the time of Whitefield's first visits and of the Great Awakening, marks the beginning of the final dissolution of the colonial state church pattern, which was to be succeeded by the emergence of the voluntary church. 1865 is a convenient watershed but, more important, it denotes here a point at which one can say that the voluntary church was securely fixed in its present form.

[3] See p. 52.

The prevailing opinion in Europe, England not excepted, has been that Religion could not be preserved without the support of Government nor Government be supported without an established religion and that there must be at least an alliance of some sort between them.

It remained for North America to bring the great and interesting subject to a fair, and finally to a decisive test.

—JAMES MADISON, 1832

Can perfect liberty and equality in religion work well when favoured by circumstances as in the United States? Is Christianity itself, in its own revelations, its own glorious platform and basis, its own provisions and divinity, when made plain, and put into the hands of a people, sufficient, without being formed and modified by the political society, to produce its legitimate fruits? This question, like many others, is in course of solution in the States.

—JAMES DIXON, 1849

THE VOLUNTARY CHURCH

I

George Whitefield

George Whitefield (1714–1770) was the leader of the "Calvinist wing" of the Methodist movement in eighteenth-century England. He was a friend of the Wesleys at Oxford and a member of the "Holy Club." After his ordination in 1736 he preached for two years in England, where, though extremely popular, he drew opposition from superiors in the Church of England because of his emphasis upon the "new birth" and his association with dissenters. In 1738 he went to Georgia, where he founded an orphanage. His frequent trips through the American colonies and the British Isles were ostensibly for the purpose of raising money for this project. His experiences were recorded in a series of journals, from which the following excerpts are taken. Whitefield's role in the Great Awakening and the effect of that movement in breaking up the colonial pattern of religious establishment are well known. Equally significant, however, is the way in which his activities in America reveal the extent to which this pattern had already been modified through force of circumstances. Though he did not often reflect upon the future of religious pluralism, he did at times approach a strikingly modern notion of ecumenical unity in evangelical effect rather than structural merger.

[*from* REVEREND MR. WHITEFIELD'S JOURNAL[1]]

Tuesday, *November* 13 [1739]. Left *Trent* Town about Six in the Morning. Had a sweet and pleasant Journey, and reached *Brunswick*, 30 Miles distant, about One. Here we were much

refreshed with the Company of Mr. *Gilbert Tennent*, an eminent
Dissenting Minister about 40 Years of Age, Son to that good old
Man who came to see me on *Saturday* at *Philadelphia*.[2] God I
find has been pleased greatly to own his Labours. He and his
Associates are now the burning and shining Lights of this Part
of *America*. He recounted to me many remarkable Effusions of
the Blessed Spirit which have been sent down amongst them; and
one may judge of their being true, faithful Soldiers of Jesus
Christ, because they are every where spoken evil of by natural
Men. The Devil, and carnal secure Ministers rage horribly against
them. Several pious Souls came to see me at his House; with
whom I took sweet Counsel. At their Request, and finding there
was a general Expectation of hearing me, *I read the Church
Liturgy*, and preached in the Evening at Mr. *Tennent's Meeting-
House.* For there is no Place set apart for the Worship of the
Church of *England*; and it is common, as I was told, in *America*,
for the Dissenters and Conformists to worship at different Times
in the same Place. *Oh that the Partition Wall was broken down,
and we all with one Heart and one Mind could glorify our
common Lord and Saviour Jesus Christ!* . . .

Thursday, November 15 [in New York]. Had several come to
see me at my Lodgings, who also gave me kind Invitations to
their Houses. Waited upon Mr. *Vessey*,[3] but could wish, for his
own Sake, he had behaved in a more Christian Manner. He
seem'd to be full of Anger and Resentment, and before I asked
him for the Use of his Pulpit, denied it. He desired to see my
Letters of Orders; I told him they were left at *Philadelphia*. He
asked me for a License. I answered I never heard that the Bishop
of *London* gave any License to any one that went to preach the
Gospel in *Georgia*, but that I was presented to the Living of
Savannah by the Trustees, and upon that Presentation had Letters
Dimissory from my Lord of *London*, which I thought was
Authority sufficient. But this was by no Means satisfactory. He
charged me with breaking my Oath, for breaking the Canon
which enjoins Ministers and Church-Wardens not to admit Persons into their Pulpit without a License. Alas! How can I break

that, when I am neither a Church-Warden, nor have any Church hereabouts to admit any one into? Upon this, hearing he was a Frequenter of Publick Houses, I reminded him of that Canon which forbids the Clergy to go to any such Places. This, tho' spoke in the Spirit of Meekness, stirr'd up his Corruptions more and more. He charged me with making a Disturbance in *Philadelphia*, and sowing and causing Divisions in other Places. But you, says he, have a Necessity laid upon you to preach; I told him I had. For the Clergy and Laity of our Church seem'd to be settled on their Lees, but my End in Preaching was not to sow Divisions, but to propagate the pure Gospel of Jesus Christ. He said they did not want my Assistance: I replied, if they did preach the Gospel, I wished them good Luck in the Name of the Lord. But as he had denied me the Church without my asking for the Use of it, I would preach in the Fields, for all Places were alike to me. Yes, says he, I find you have been used to that. After this, he taxed me with censuring my Superiors. I told him I was no Respecter of Persons; if a Bishop committed a Fault, I would tell him of it; if a common Clergyman did not act aright, I would be free with him also, as well as with a Layman. . . .

Tuesday, November 20. Reached hither [New Brunswick] about Six last Night, and preached about Noon, for near Two Hours, in worthy Mr. *Tennent's* Meeting-House, to a large Assembly gather'd together from all Parts; and amongst them, as Mr. *Tennent* told me, there was a great Body of solid Christians. About Three in the Afternoon, I preach'd again, and at Seven I baptized two Children, and preached a third Time with greater Freedom than at either of the former Opportunities. It is impossible to tell with what Pleasure the Children of God heard those Truths confirm'd by a Minister of the Church of *England*, which for many Years have been preached to them by their own Pastor. Mr. *Tennent's* Opposers Mouths were stopt, several were brought under strong Convictions, and our Lord's dear Disciples were ready to leap for Joy. To me the Meeting seemed to be like the Meeting of the Twelve Tribes, when they came from different Parts to worship the Lord at *Jerusalem*. Among others that came to hear the Word, were several Ministers whom the Lord has been pleased to honour, in making Instruments to bringing many Sons of Glory. One was a *Dutch* Calvinistical Minister, named *Freeling Housen*,[4] Pastor of a Congregation about Four Miles off *New Brunswick*; he is a worthy old Soldier of Jesus Christ, and was the Beginner of the great Work which I trust the Lord is carrying on in these Parts. He has been strongly opposed by his carnal Brethren, but God has always appeared for him in a surprising Manner, and made him more than Conqueror, thro' his Love. He has long since learnt to fear him *only* who can destroy both Body and Soul in Hell. Another was one Mr. *Cross*, Minister of a Congregation at *Barking-Bridge*, about Twenty Miles from *Brunswick*. A most remarkable Out-pouring of the Spirit has been frequently *seen* in his Assembly, for which he has been opposed much by natural Men. He himself told me of many wonderful Effects, and sudden Conversions that had been wrought by the Lord under his Ministry. For some Time Eight or Nine used to come to him together, in deep Distress of Soul; and I think he said, Three Hundred of his Congregation, which is not very large, were effectually brought Home to Christ; but tho' they are the excellent ones of the Earth, they are look'd upon as Enthusiasts and Madmen, and treated as such by those who know not God, and are ignorant of the hidden Life of Jesus Christ in their Hearts. He indeed is one who I believe would rejoice to suffer for the Lord Jesus. Oh! that I may be like minded! A Third Minister was one Mr. *Camel*, who has been a Preacher of the Doctrines of Grace for these Four Years, was a regular moral Liver, and accounted a very good Man, but within these few Months being convinced of Sin, and that he knew nothing experimentally of Jesus Christ, tho' he had pretended to preach him so long, after many Struggles with himself, he told the Synod he was unconverted, and therefore dared not preach 'till he was; accordingly, he has left off preaching these Two Months, and has labour'd under unspeakable Anguish and Distress of Soul. By some he is look'd upon as melancholy, and besides himself; but I had much Discourse with him, and really believe these Humiliations will prepare him for great and eminent

Services in the Church of God. His Case puts me in Mind of Professor *Frank*, who being on *Easter-Day* to preach on the Nature of Divine Faith, and finding he had not that Faith himself, was convicted by God of his unregenerate State, upon which he ran into the Woods, was there deeply humbled, and at last became a most exalted Instance of Faith. At our Persuasion, Mr. *Camel* promised to preach next *Sunday*, and I believe will be instrumental in convicting many Heart Hypocrites among the Dissenting Ministers. For that there are many such is evident from this:—tho' they hold, and have been bred up in, and preach the Doctrines of Grace, yet whenever the Power of God appears in any Congregation, they cry it down as much as our Ministers of the Church of *England*. *Oh that the Lord may comfort poor Mr. Camel, and cause him to detect these Wolves in Sheep's Cloathing!* With these Ministers, and many other Disciples of our dear Lord Jesus, I took sweet Counsel; we eat our Bread with Gladness and Singleness of Heart, and comforted ourselves with this Consideration, that tho' we must be separated from each other on Earth, yet we should sit down to eat Bread with *Abraham*, *Isaac*, and *Jacob*, in the Kingdom of Heaven. *Hasten, O Lord, this blessed Time! Oh when will thy Kingdom come!* . . .

Thursday, November 22. Set out for *Neshamini* (twenty Miles distant from *Trent Town*) where old Mr. *Tennent* lives, and keeps an Academy, and where I was to preach to Day, according to Appointment. About Twelve we came thither, and found above 3000 People gather'd together in the Meeting-House Yard; and Mr. *William Tennent*, and eminent Servant of Jesus Christ, preaching to them, because we had stayed beyond the Time appointed. When I came up, he soon stopp'd, and sung a Psalm, and then I began to speak as the Lord gave me Utterance. At first the People seem'd unaffected, but in the midst of my Discourse, the Power of the Lord Jesus came upon me, and I felt such a Struggling within myself for the People, as I scarce ever felt before. The Hearers began to be melted down immediately, and cry much; and we had good Reason to hope the Lord intended Good for many. After I had finished, Mr. *Gilbert Tennent* gave a Word of Exhortation to confirm what had been deliver'd. At the End of his Discourse, we sung a Psalm, and then dismiss'd the People with a Blessing. *Oh that the Lord may say Amen to it!* After our Exercises were over, we went to old Mr. *Tennent*, who entertain'd us like cne of the ancient Patriarchs. His Wife to me seemed like *Elizabeth*, and he like *Zaccbary*; both as far as I can find, walk in all the Ordinances and Commandments of the Lord blameless. Tho' God was pleased to humble my Soul, so that I was obliged to retire for a while, yet we had sweet Communion with each other, and spent the Evening in concerting what Measures had best be taken for promoting our dear Lord's Kingdom. It happens very providentially, that Mr. *Tennent* and his Brethren are appointed to be a Presbytery by the Synod, so that they intend breeding up gracious Youths, and sending them out from Time to Time into our Lord's Vineyard. The Place wherein the young Men study now is in Contempt call'd *the College*. It is a Log-House, about Twenty Feet long, and near as many broad; and to me it seemed to resemble the Schools of the old Prophets. For that their Habitations were mean, and that they sought not great Things for themselves, is plain from that Passage of Scripture wherein we are told, that at the Feast of the Sons of the Prophets, one of them put on the Pot, whilst the others went to fetch some Herbs out of the Field. All that can be said of most of our publick Universities is, they are all glorious *without*. From this despised Place Seven or Eight worthy Ministers of Jesus have lately been sent forth; more are almost ready to be sent, and a Foundation is now laying for the Instruction of many others. The Devil will certainly rage against them, but the Work, I am persuaded, is of God, and therefore will not come to nought. Carnal Ministers oppose them strongly; and because People, when awaken'd by Mr. *Tennent*, or his Brethren, see through, and therefore leave their Ministry, the poor Gentlemen are loaded with Contempt, and look'd upon (as all faithful Preachers will be) as Persons that turn the World upside down. A notable War I believe is commencing between *Michael* and the Dragon, we can easily guess who will prevail. *The Seed of the Woman shall bruise the Serpent's Head.* . . .

Tuesday, November 27. According to Appointment, preached

at *German Town*, seven Miles from *Philadelphia*, off a Balcony, to above 6000 People. Before I began I retired, and was humbled at the Throne of Grace. But God strengthened me to speak very near two Hours with such Demonstration of the Spirit, that great Numbers continued weeping for a considerable Time. I have not seen a more gracious Melting for a long Season. After I had done, People came to me shaking me by the Hand, and inviting me to their Houses, and fresh Places. A *German* most kindly entertain'd me. I had sweet Converse, and felt a blessed Union and Communion with many Souls, though of different Nations and Professions. I think there are no less than fifteen particular Denominations of Christians in *German Town*, and yet all agree in one Thing, that is, to hold Jesus Christ as their Head, and to worship him in Spirit and in Truth. I talked with one who had been banished out of *Switzerland* for preaching Christ, and Numbers are scattered round about the Town who were driven out of their native Countries for the Sake of their Holy Religion. . . .

About eight in the Evening we reached *Philadelphia*, and found great Numbers waiting round my Door to hear the Word of Life. After I had paid a Visit, and talked closely to two Persons who were doubting of the Principles of the Quakers, I returned home; and though I was weak, I could not bear to let so many Souls go away without a Spiritual Morsel; I therefore gave them a Word of Exhortation, as the Spirit gave me Utterance, sung a Hymn, prayed and dismissed them with a Blessing. Many wept bitterly, and the People's Behaviour more and more convinces me that God has begun a good Work in many Souls. Was there proper Encouragement given, I am persuaded *Georgia* might soon be peopled; many would gladly go with me thither. I cannot but hope that it will be in Time a fruitful Soil for Christians. One great Reason, I believe, why *Pensilvania* flourishes above other Provinces, is the Liberty of Conscience which is given all to worship God in their own Way; by this means, it is as it were an Asylum or Place of Refuge for all persecuted Christians; and methinks they live here as so many Guardian Angels. I want to go up in the Woods to see more of them, but Time will not permit. O when shall the Children of God sit down together in the Kingdom of their Father! There we shall all speak *one Language*, and join in singing the Song of the Lamb for ever! *Lord make my Soul to thirst more and more after that blissful Communion of Saints!* . . .

Monday, August 24 [Charlestown]. Being but weak in Body (except on *Sundays*) I have preached only once every Day: But I think with greater Power than ever, and with greater Success. I scarce know the Time, wherein I did not see a considerable melting in some Part or other of the Congregation, and often it spread over all the Parts of it. Several Times I was so weak before I began to preach, that I thought it almost impossible I should go through half a Discourse. But the Lord quickened, enlightened, and supported me above Measure. Out of Weakness, I became strong, and the Lord manifested himself in the Sanctuary. The Audiences were more numerous than ever, and it was supposed, not less than 4000 were in and about the Meeting-house, when I preached my Farewel-Sermon. The Commissary,[5] having run his utmost Length, thought it best to say no more himself; finding, when I was here last, that Jesus Christ was not preached in the Church, my Conscience would not suffer me to attend on those that preached there any more. I therefore went to the Baptist and Independent Meeting-houses, where Jesus Christ was preached in Sincerity. I likewise administered the Sacrament thrice in a private House, Yesterday, Yesterday was seven-night, and this Morning. Never did I see any Thing more solemn. The Room was large, and most dissolved into Tears, as tho' they were weeping at their Saviour's Cross. Surely Jesus Christ crucified was evidently set forth before them. Many, at their Request, stood by that did not receive, but they wept bitterly. I prayed for them all with great Power, and I hope the Lord will cloath them with a Wedding Garment. What was best, Baptists, Church Folks and Presbyterians, all joined together, and received according to the Church of *England*, except two, who desired to have it sitting: I willingly complied, knowing it was a Thing quite indifferent. . . .

[Friday, September 19, 1740, at Boston.] At eleven I went to publick Worship at the Church of *England*, and afterwards went home with the Commissary,[6] who read Prayers. He received me very courteously, and it being a Day whereon the Clergy of the established Church met, I had an Opportunity of conversing with five of them together. I think, one of them began with me for calling "*That Tennent* and his Brethren *faithful* Ministers of Jesus Christ." I answered, "I believed they were." They then questioned me about "the Validity of the Presbyterian Ordination." I replied, "I believed it was valid." They then urged against me a Passage in my first Journal, where I said, "That a Baptist Minister at *Deal* did not give a satisfactory Answer concerning his Mission." I answered, "Perhaps my Sentiments were altered." "And is Mr. *Wesley* altered, said one, in his Sentiments? For he was very strenuous for the Church, and rigorous against all other Forms of Government when he was at *Boston*." I answered, "He was then a great Bigot, but God has since enlarged his Heart, and I believed he was now like-minded with me in this Particular." I then urged, "That a Catholic Spirit was best, and that a Baptist-Minister had communicated lately with me at *Savannah*." And, "I suppose, says another, you would do him as good a Turn, and would communicate with him." I answered, "Yes." I then urged, "That it was best to preach up the New Birth, and the Power of Godliness, and not to insist so much upon the Form: For People would never be brought to one Mind as to that; nor did Jesus Christ ever intend it." "Yes, but, says Doctor *Cutler*,[7] he did." "How do you prove it." Why, says he, "Christ prayed, *That all might be one, even as thou Father and I are one*." I replied, "That was spoken of the inward Union of the Souls of Believers with Jesus Christ, and not of the outward Church." "That cannot be, says Dr. *Cutler*, for how then could it be said, *That the World might know that thou hast sent me?*" He then (taking it for granted that the Church of *England* was the only true Apostolical Church) drew a Parallel between the *Jewish* and our Church, urging how God required all Things to be made according to the Pattern given in the Mount. I answered, "That before the Parallel could be just, it must be proved, that every Thing enjoin'd in our Church was as much of a divine Institution as any Rite or

Ceremony under the *Jewish* Dispensation." I added further, "That I saw regenerate Souls among the Baptists, among the Presbyterians, among the Independents, and among the Church-Folks, all Children of God, and yet all born again in a different Way of Worship, and who can tell which is most evangelical?" . . .

[Whitefield pauses at the conclusion of his New England tour.]

But here I think it proper to set up my *Ebenezer*, before I enter into the Province of *New-York*, to give God Thanks for sending me to *New-England*. "I have now had an Opportunity of seeing the greatest and most populous Part of it, and take it all together, it certainly on many Accounts exceeds all other Provinces in *America*, and, for the Establishment of Religion, perhaps all other Parts of the World. Never surely was a Place so well settled in so short a Time. The Towns all through *Connecticut* and Eastward towards *York*, in the Province of *Massachusetts*, near the River-side, are large, well peopled, and exceeding pleasant to travel through. Every five Miles, or perhaps less, you have a Meeting-House, and, I believe, there is no such Thing as a Pluralist or Non-resident Minister in both Provinces. Many, nay most that preach, I fear do not experimentally know Christ; yet I cannot see much worldly Advantage to tempt them to take upon them the sacred Function. . . . The Church of *England* is at a low Ebb, and, as far as I can find, had People kept their Primitive Purity, it would scarce have got Footing in *New-England*. I have many Evidences to prove that most of the Churches have been first set up by immoral Men, and such as would not submit to the Discipline of their Congregations. But I'll say no more of the poor Church of *England*. Most of her Sons, I fear, hate to be reformed, and will but cast my Words behind them. As for the Civil Government of *New-England*, it seems to be well regulated, and I think, at opening all their Courts, either the Judge or a Minister begins with a Prayer. Family Worship, I believe, is generally kept up. The Negroes, I think better used in respect both to Soul and Body, than in any other Province I have yet seen: In short, I like *New-England* exceeding well; and when a Spirit of Reformation revives, it certainly will prevail more than in any other Place, because they are simple in their Worship, less corrupt in their Principles, and consequently easier to be brought over to the Form of sound Words, into which so many of their pious Ancestors were delivered." *Send forth, O Lord, thy Light and thy Truth, and for thy infinite Mercy's Sake, shew thou hast a peculiar Delight in those habitable Parts of the Earth! Amen, Lord Jesus, Amen and Amen!*

NOTES

[1] Complete bibliographic information is listed on pp. 193–5.

[2] The Tennents were chiefly responsible for the onset of the Great Awakening among Presbyterians in the middle colonies. William Tennent (1673–1745?) established the "Log College" in Bucks County, Pennsylvania, where a number of young men, including three of his sons, were trained for the ministry. Of these Gilbert Tennent (1703–1764) was most prominent in his use of evangelical and revivalistic methods. The controversy aroused by his ministry culminated in a schism a year after this meeting with Whitefield.

[3] William Vessey (d. 1746) was rector of Trinity Church, the first Anglican parish in New York.

[4] Theodorus Jacobus Frelinghuysen (1691–1747) was a minister of the Dutch Reformed Church who served several parishes in New Jersey. His use of the methods associated with the Great Awakening began as early as 1720.

[5] There were no Anglican bishops in America throughout the colonial period. Episcopal authority for the colonies was exercised by the Bishop of London. After 1675 certain administrative powers were delegated to colonial officials who were called commissaries. The commissary at Charleston at this time was Alexander Garden.

[6] Roger Price, rector of Kings Chapel from 1730 to 1748, also served as commissary for New England.

[7] Timothy Cutler (1684–1765) was ordained in the Congregational Church and was rector at Yale from 1718 to 1722. He later became an Anglican, was ordained in London in 1723 and became rector of Christ Church in Boston. He was noted, among other things, for his intolerance of Dissenters.

2

Alexander Hamilton

Alexander Hamilton (1712–1756) was a Scottish physician who spent the greater portion of his life in Maryland. He was educated at Edinburgh and received the doctor of medicine degree in 1737. Two years later he came to Annapolis, where an older brother had already settled. Hamilton's medical skills were rare in the American colonies, and he quickly became a prosperous and influential member of Maryland society. He married into one of the most prominent families in the colony, was elected to the legislature, and joined the Church of England. His travels through New England and the middle colonies were made in 1744, five years after his arrival. His account is that of an educated European sophisticate who looked with rather detached amusement at the natural, social, and religious curiosities he encountered.

[*from* GENTLEMAN'S PROGRESS]

I CROSSED Bohemia Ferry and lodged att the ferry house. The landlord's name I cannot remember, but he seemed to be a man of tollerable parts for one in his station. Our conversation run chiefly upon religion. He gave me a short account of the spirit of enthusiasm that had lately possessed the inhabitants of the forrests there and informed me that it had been a common practise for companys of 20 or 30 hair brained fanaticks to ride thro' the woods singing of psalms. I went to bed att 9 att night; my landlord, his wife, daughters, and I lay all in one room.

Saturday, June 2d. In the morning there was a clear sky over head but a foggy horizon and the wind att south, which presaging heat, I set out very early. . . .

I dined att a tavern with a very mixed company of different nations and religions. There were Scots, English, Dutch, Germans, and Irish; there were Roman Catholicks, Church men, Presbyterians, Quakers, Newlightmen, Methodists, Seventh day men, Moravians, Anabaptists, and one Jew. The whole company consisted of 25 planted round an oblong table in a great hall well stoked with flys. The company divided into comittees in conversation; the prevailing topick was politicks and conjectures of a French war. A knott of Quakers there talked only about selling of flower and the low price it bore. They touched a little upon religion, and high words arose among some of the sectaries, but their blood was not hot enough to quarrell, or, to speak in the canting phraze, their zeal wanted fervency. A gentleman that sat next me proposed a number of questions concerning Maryland, understanding I had come from thence. In my replys I was reserved, pretending to know little of the matter as being a person whose business did not lye in the way of history and politicks. . . .

The Quakers here [Philadelphia] have two large meetings, the Church of England one great church in Second Street, and another built for Whitefield in which one Tennent, a fanatick, now preaches, the Romans one chapell, the Anabaptists one or two meetings, and the Presbyterians two.

The Quakers are the richest and the people of greatest interest in this government; of them their House of Assembly is chiefly composed. They have the character of an obstinate, stiff necked generation and a perpetuall plague to their governors. The present governour, Mr. Thomas, has fallen upon a way to manage them better than any of his predecessors did and, att the same time, keep pritty much in their good graces and share some of their favours. However, the standing or falling of the Quakers in the House of Assembly depends upon their making sure the interest of the Palatines in this province, who of late have turned so numerous that they can sway the votes which way they please.

Here is no publick magazine of arms nor any method of defence, either for city or province, in case of the invasion of an enemy. This is owing to the obstinacy of the Quakers in maintaining their principle of non-resistance. It were a pity but they were put to a sharp triall to see whether they would act as they profess.

I never was in a place so populous where the gout for publick gay diversions prevailed so little. There is no such thing as assemblys of the gentry among them, either for dancing or musick; these they have had an utter aversion to ever since Whitefield preached among them. Their chief employ, indeed, is traffick and mercantile business which turns their thoughts from these levitys. Some Virginia gentlemen that came here with the Commissioners of the Indian Treaty were desirous of having a ball but could find none of the feemale sex in a humour for it. Strange influence of religious enthusiasm upon human nature to excite an aversion at these innocent amusements, for the most part so agreeable and entertaining to the young and gay, and indeed, in the opinion of moderate people, so conducive to the improvement of politeness, good manners, and humanity. . . .

I put up att one Eliah Bond's att the Sign of the Wheat Sheaf [in Trenton, New Jersey]. Two gentlemen of the town came there and invited me into their company. One was named Cadwaller,[1] a doctor in the place and, as I understood, a fallen off Quaker. We supped upon cold gammon and a sallet. Our discourse was mixed and rambling; att first it was politicall; then Cadwaller gave me the character of the constitution and government. The House of Assembly here, he told me, was chiefly composed of mechanicks and ignorant wretches, obstinate to the last degree; that there were a number of proprietors in the government, and a multitude of Quakers. He enlarged a little in the praise of Governour Morris,[2] who is now a very old man. From politicks the discourse turned to religion and then to physick.

Cadwaller asked me concerning severall people in Maryland, and among the rest (not yet knowing me) he came across my self, asking me if Hamilton att Annapolis was dead or alive. "Here he is," says I, "bodily and not spiritually." He told me the reason why he enquired was that about a twelvemonth agoe, one Dr. Thomson from Maryland had been there and had reported he was going to settle att Annapolis in place of Hamilton there who they did not expect would live. "But, sir," says he, "if you be the man, I congratulate you upon your unexpected recovery."

Thus passing from one subject to another in discourse, Cadwaller inveighed bitterly against the idle ceremonies that had been foisted into religious worship by almost all sects and perswasions—not that there was any thing materiall in these ceremonies to cavill att providing the true design of them was understood and they were esteemed only as decent decorations and ornaments to divine service in the temples and churches, but upon account that the vulgar in all ages had been misled and imposed upon by wicked, politick, and designing priests and perswaded that the strength and sinews of religion lay in such fopperies, and that there was no such thing as being a good man or attaining salvation without all this trumpery. "It is certain," added he, "that a superstitious regard and veneration to the mere ceremonials of religion has contributed very much to corrupt the manners of men, turning their thoughts from true morality and virtue (to promote which ought to be the sole aim of all religions whatsoever) to dwell upon dreams, chimeras fit only to distract the human mind and give place for mad zeal, the woefull author of persecution, murder, and cruelty."

To this I replied that priests of all sorts and sects whatsoever made a kind of trade of religion, contriving how to make it turn out to their own gain and profit; yet notwithstanding, many were of opinion that to inculcate religion into vulgar minds we must use other methods than only preaching up fine sense and morality to them. Their understanding and comprehension are too gross and thick to receive it in that shape. Men of sense of every perswasion whatsoever are sensible of the emptiness and nonsense of the mere cermonial part of religion but, att the same time, allow it to be in some degree necessary and usefull, because the ignorant vulgar are to be dealt with in this point as we manage children by showing them toys in order to perswade them to do that which all the good reasoning of the world never would. The mobile, that many headed beast, cannot be reasoned into religious and pious duties. Men are not all philosophers. The tools by which we must work upon the gross senses and rough cast minds of the vulgar are such as form and lay before their eyes, rewards and punishments whereby the passions of hope and fear are excited; and withall our doctrines must be interlaced with something amazing and misterious in order to command their attention, strengthen their belief, and raise their admiration, for was one to make religion appear to them in her genuine, simple, and plain dress, she would gain no credit and would never be so regarded. Here Cadwaller interupted me and said all these discourses signified nothing, for he thought she was very little regarded even as it was. We dismissed att twelve att night. . . .

Att half an hour after eight in the morning, I put up at one Leonards's aat the Sign of the Black Lyon in Kingstown, another small village upon the road. I breakfasted there upon a dish of tea and was served by a pritty smiling girl, the landlord's daughter. After breakfast, as I sat in the porch, there arrived a waggon with some company. There were in it two Irishman, a Scotsman, and a Jew. The Jew's name was Abraham Du-bois, a French man by birth. He spoke such bad English that I could scarce understand him. He told me he had been att Conestogo to visit some relations he had there; that he left that place upon Monday last, and att that time there had arrived there 40 canoes of Indians of the tribes of the Mohooks and 5 Nations going to treat with the Governours and Commissioners of the American provinces.

This Jew and the company that were with him begun a dispute about sacred history. He insisted much upon the books of Moses and the authority of the Old Testament. He asked the Scotsman in particular if he believed the Old Testament. He replied that now a days there were few Old Testament people, all having become *New Light men*, "for," says he, "among the Christians, one wife is sufficient for one man, but your Old Testament fornicators were allowed a plurality of wives and as many concubines as they could afford to maintain." The Jew made no answer to this nonsensicall reply but began very wisely to settle what day of the week it was and what time of that day that God began the creation of the world. He asserted that it was upon the day that the Christians call Sunday, and that when the light first appeared, it was in the west, and therefor it was in the evening that the creation was begun. "Had that evening no morning then?" replied the Scotsman with a sneer. To which the Jew answered that there had been no dawn or sun rising that day because the sun was not yet created to run his diurnall course, but that a glorious stream of light suddenly appeared by the mandate of God in the west. "I never heard of an evening without a morning in my life before," replied his antagonist, "and it is nonsence to suppose any such thing." "Cannot black exist," said the Jew, "without its opposite white?" "It may be so," said the Scotsman, "but why does your countryman Moses say 'and the evening and the morning was the first day'?" The Jew answered that the evening was there first mentioned because the work was begun upon the evening, att which the Scotsman swore that the words were misplaced by the translators, which pert reply put an end to the dispute. . . .

Sunday, June 24th. At four in the morning, Mr. Milne and I went ashore to the taveren, and there we met with a justice of the peace and a New Light taylor. The justice seemed to have the greatest half or all the learning of the county in his face, but so soon as he spoke, we found that he was no more learned than other men. The taylor's phizz was screwed up to a santified pitch, and he seemed to be either under great sorrow for his sins or else a hatching some mischief in his heart, for I have heard that your hipocriticall rogues always put on their most solemn countenance or vizzard when they are contriving how to perpetrate their villanies. We soon discovered that this taylor was a Moravian. The Moravians are a wild, fanatick sect with which both this place and the Jerseys are pestered. They live in common, men and women mixed in a great house or barn where they sometimes eat and drink, sometimes sleep, and sometimes preach and howl, but are quite idle and will employ themselves in no usefull work. They think all things should be in common and say that religion is intirely corrupted by being too much blended with the laws of the country. They call their religion the true religion, or the religion of the Lamb, and they commonly term themselves the followers of the Lamb, which I believe is true in so far as some of them may be wolves in sheep's clothing. This sect was first founded by a German enthusiast, Count Zenzindorff, who used to go about some years agoe and perswade the people to his opinions and drop a certain catechism which he had published upon the high way. They received a considerable strength and addition to their number by Whitefield's preaching in these parts but now are upon the decline since there is no opposition made to them.[3] Milne and I anatomized this Moravian taylor in his own hearing, and yet he did not know of it, for we spoke Latin. He asked what language that was. The justice told him he believed it was Latin, att which the cabbager sigh'd and said it was a pagan language. We treated him, however, with a dram and went from the taveren to one Cardevitz's who, havint the rheumatism in his arm, asked my advice, which I gave him. The land here is high and woody, and the air very cool. . . .

Our conversation run upon the enthusiasm now prevalent in these parts and the strange madness that had possessed some people att Ipswitch occasioned by one Woodberry, a mad enthusiast, who, pretending to inspiration, uttered severall blasphemous and absurd speeches, asserting that he was the same to day, yesterday, and for ever, saying he had it in his power to save or damn whom he pleased, falling down upon the ground, licking the dust, and condemning all to hell who would not do the like, drinking healths to King Jesus, the self existing Being, and prosperity to the kingdom of heaven, and a thousand other such mad and ridiculous frolicks. I was quite shoked att these relations, both when I heard them mentioned in conversation and saw them published in the news paper, being surprized that some of the chief clergy there had been so weak as to be drawn away be these follies. This is a remarkable instance to what lengths of madness enthusiasm will carry men once they give it a loose rein, and tho' excursions may appear shoking to people in their senses, yet so much good may follow them as that the interest and influence of these fanatick preachers will be thereby depressed among all such people as are not quite fools or mad. These extravagancies take all their first root from the labours of that righteous apostle Whitefield who, only for the sake of private lucre and gain, sowed the first seeds of distraction in these unhappy, ignorant parts.

NOTES

[1] Thomas Cadwalader (1707–1799) was a prominent Philadelphia physician. After 1738 he lived on his father-in-law's estate near Trenton, New Jersey.

[2] Lewis Morris (1671–1746) was chief justice of the New York Supreme Court from 1715 to 1733. In 1738 he became governor of New Jersey.

[3] There is no basis for this attack on the Moravians other than Hamilton's credulity in all matters which tended to discredit religious enthusiasm. The Moravians traced their origins to followers of John Huss in the fifteenth century. In order to escape persecution, early in the eighteenth century they took refuge on the Saxony estate of Nicholas Ludwig, Count von Zinzendorf (1700–1760). Zinzendorf soon accepted their evangelical doctrines and became their leader. In 1741 he came to America and assisted in establishing the Moravian settlement at Bethlehem, Pennsylvania.

3

Peter Kalm

To many European men of science the most exciting thing
about the discovery of America was the existence of two vast
continents, each larger than Europe, teeming with unsuspected
varieties of plant and animal life. Peter Kalm (1716–1779), the
Swedish botanist, was one of those fortunate enough to make
his observations at first hand. His close friend the renowned
Linnaeus recommended to the Swedish government that he be
sent to North America for three years to make a survey of its
natural history. Kalm was in America from 1748 to 1751, and
a three volume account of his travels was published the year
following his return. In 1770 an English translation was published as *Travels into North America*. Happily, Kalm recorded
his observations of social as well as natural phenomena. The
affair of Rev. Slaughter and his rival, for example, like so many
of the flora and fauna Kalm encountered, could have taken
place "only in America."

[*from* TRAVELS INTO NORTH AMERICA]

Among the publick buildings [in Philadelphia] I will first
mention churches, of which there are several, for God is served
in various ways in this country.

The *English established church* stands in the northern part of
the town, at some distance from the market, and is the finest
of all. It has a little, inconsiderable steeple, in which is a bell to
be rung when it is time to go to church, and on burials. It has
likewise a clock which strikes the hours. This building which is

called Christ church, was founded towards the end of the last century, but has lately been rebuilt and more adorned. It has two ministers who get the greatest part of their salary from *England*. In the beginning of this century, the *Swedish* minister, the Rev. Mr. *Rudmann*, performed the functions of a clergyman to the *English* congregation for near two years, during the absence of their own clergyman.

The *Swedish church*, which is otherwise called the church of *Weekacko*, is on the southern part of the town, and almost without it, on the river's side, and its situation is therefore more agreeable than that of any other. I shall have an opportunity of describing it more exactly, when I shall speak of the *Swedes* in particular, who live in this place.

The *German Lutheran church*, is on the north-west side of the town. On my arrival in *America* it had a little steeple, but that being put up by an ignorant architect, before the walls of the church were quite dry, they leaned forwards by its weight, and therefore they were forced to pull it down again in the autumn of the year 1750. About that time the congregation received a fine organ from *Germany*. They have only one minister, who likewise preaches at another Lutheran church in *Germantown*. He preaches alternately one sunday in that church, and another in this. The first clergyman which the Lutherans had in this town, was the Rev. Mr. *Muhlenberg*,[1] who laid the foundations of this church in 1743, and being called to another place afterwards, the Rev. Mr. *Brunholz* from *Sleswick* was his successor, and is yet here. Both these gentlemen were sent to this place from *Hall* in *Saxony*, and have been a great advantage to it by their peculiar talent of preaching in an edifying manner. A little while before this church was built, the *Lutheran Germans* had no clergyman for themselves, so that the every-where beloved *Swedish* minister at *Weekacko*, Mr. *Dylander*, preached likewise to them. He therefore preached three sermons every sunday; the first early in the morning to the *Germans*; the second to the *Swedes*, and the third in the afternoon to the *English*, and besides this he went all the week into the country and instructed the *Germans* who lived separately there. He therefore frequently preached sixteen sermons a week. And after his death, which happened in *November* 1741, the *Germans* first wrote to *Germany* for a clergyman for themselves. This congregation is at present very numerous, so that every sunday the church is very much crowded. It has two galleries, but no vestry. They do not sing the collects, but read them before the altar.

The *old Presbyterian church*, is not far from the market, and on the south-side of *market-street*. It is of a middling size, and built in the year 1704, as the inscription on the northern pediment shews. The roof is built almost hemispherical, or at least forms a hexagon. The whole building stands from north to south, for the presbyterians do not regard, as other people do, whether their churches look towards a certain point of the heavens or not.

The *new Presbyterian church* was built in the year 1750, by the *New-lights* in the north-western part of the town. By the name of *New-lights*, are understood the people who have, from different religions, become proselytes to the well known *Whitefield*, who in the years 1739, 1740, and likewise in 1744 and 1745 travelled through almost all the *English* colonies. His delivery, his extraordinary zeal, and other talents so well adapted to the intelects of his hearers, made him so popular that he frequently, especially in the two first years, got from eight thousand to twenty thousand hearers in the fields. His intention in these travels, was to collect money for an orphans hospital which had been erected in *Georgia*. He here frequently collected seventy pounds sterling at one sermon; nay, at two sermons which he preached in the year 1740, both on one sunday, at *Philadelphia*, he got an hundred and fifty pounds. The proselytes of this man, or the above-mentioned *New-lights*, are at present merely a sect of presbyterians. For though *Whitefield* was originally a clergyman of the *English* church, yet he deviated by little and little from her doctrines; and on arriving in the year 1744 at *Boston* in *New England*, he disputed with the Presbyterians about their doctrines, so much that he almost entirely embraced them. For *Whitefield* was no great disputant, and could therefore easily be led by these cunning people, whithersoever they would have him. This likewise during his latter stay in *America* caused his audience to be less numerous than during the first. The *New-lights* built first in the year 1741, a great house in the western part of the town, to hold divine service in. But a division arising amongst them after the departure of *Whitefield*, and besides on other accounts, the building was sold to the town in the beginning of the year 1750, and destined for a school. The *New-lights* then built a church which I call the *new Presbyterian* one. On its eastern pediment is the following inscription, in golden letters: *Templum Presbyterianum, annuente numine, erectum, Anno Dom. MDCCI.*

The *old German reformed church* is built in the west north-west part of the town, and looks like the church in the *Ladugoord-field* near *Stockholm*. It is not yet finished, though for several years together, the congregation has kept up divine service in it. These *Germans* attended the *German* service at the *Swedish* church, whilst the *Swedish* minister Mr. *Dylander* lived. But as the *Lutherans* got a clergyman for themselves on the death of the last, those of the reformed church made likewise preparations to get one from *Dordrecht*; and the first who was sent to them, was the Rev. Mr. *Slaughter*, whom I found on my arrival. But in the year 1750, another clergyman of the reformed church arrived from *Holland*, and by his artful behaviour, so insinuated himself into the favour of the Rev. Mr. *Slaughter's* congregation, that the latter lost almost half his audience. The two clergymen then disputed for several sundays together, about the pulpit, nay, people relate that the new comer mounted the pulpit on a saturday, and stayed in it all night. The other being thus excluded, the two parties in the audience made themselves the subject both of the laughter and of the scorn of the whole town by beating and bruising each other, and committing other excesses. The affair was inquired into by the magistrates, and decided in favour of the Rev. Mr. *Slaughter*, the person who had been abused.

The *new reformed church*, was built at a little distance from the old one by the party of the clergyman, who had lost his cause.

This man however had influence enough to bring over to his party almost the whole audience of his antagonist, at the end of the year 1750, and therefore this new church will soon be useless.

The *Quakers* have two meetings, one in the market, and the other in the northern part of the town. In them are according to the custom of this people, neither altars, nor pulpits, nor any other ornaments usual in churches; but only seats and some sconces. They meet thrice every sunday in them, and besides that at certain times every week or every month. I shall mention more about them hereafter.

The Baptists have their service in the northern part of the town.

The *Roman Catholicks* have in the south-west part of the town a great house, which is well adorned within, and has an organ.

The *Moravian Brethren* have hired a great house, in the northern part of the town, in which they performed the service both in *German* and in *English*; not only twice or three times every sunday, but likewise every night after it was grown dark. But in the winter of the year 1750, they were obliged to drop their evening meetings; some wanton young fellows having several times disturbed the congregation, by an instrument sounding like the note of a cuckoo, for this noise they made in a dark corner, not only at the end of every stanza, but likewise at that of every line, whilst they were singing a hymn. . . .

All persons who intend to be married, must either have their banns published three times from the pulpit, or get a licence from the governor. The banns of the poorer sort of people only are published, and all those who are a little above them get a licence from the governor. In that licence he declares that he has examined the affair, and found no obstacles to hinder the marriage, and therefore he allows it. The licence is signed by the governor; but, before he delivers it, the bridegroom must come to him in company with two creditable and well known men, who answer for him, that there really is no lawful obstacle to his marriage. These men must subscribe a certificate, in which they make themselves answerable for, and engage to bear all the damages of, any complaints made by the relations of the persons who intend to be married, by their guardians, their masters, or by those to whom they may have been promised before. For all these circumstances the governor cannot possibly know. They further certify that nothing hinders the intended marriage, and that nothing is to be feared on that account. For a licence they pay five and twenty shillings in *Pensylvanian* money, at *Philadelphia*. The governor keeps twenty shillings, or one pound, and the remaining five shillings belong to his secretary. The licence is directed only to protestant clergymen. The quakers have a peculiar licence to their marriages. But as it would be very troublesome, especially for those who live far from the governor's residence to come up to town for every licence, and to bring the men with them who are to answer for them, the clergymen in the country commonly take a sufficient number of licences and certificates, which are ready printed, with blanks left for the names; they give them occasionally, and get the common money, one pound, five shillings, for each of them, besides something for their trouble. The money that they have collected, they deliver to the governor as soon as they come to town, together with the certificates, which are signed by two men, as above-mentioned; they then take again as many licences as they think sufficient: from hence we may conceive that the governors in the *English North American* colonies, besides their salaries, have very considerable revenues.

There is a great mixture of people of all sorts in these colonies, partly of such as are lately come over from *Europe*, and partly of such as have not yet any settled place of abode. Hence it frequently happens that when a clergyman has married such a couple, the bridegroom says he has no money at present, but would pay the fee at the first opportunity: however he goes off with his wife, and the clergyman never gets his due. This proceeding has given occasion to a custom which is now common in *Maryland*. When the clergyman marries a very poor couple, he breaks off in the middle of the Liturgy, and cries out, *Where is my fee?* The man must then give the money, and the clergyman proceeds; but if the bridegroom has no money, the clergyman defers the marriage till another time, when the man is better provided. People of fortune, of whom the clergyman is sure to get his due, need not fear this disagreeable question, when they are married.

However, though the parson has got licences to marry a couple, yet if he be not very careful, he may get into very disagreeable circumstances; for in many parts of the country there is a law made, which, notwithstanding the governor's licence, greatly limits a clergyman in some cases. He is not allowed to marry a couple who are not yet of age, unless he be certain of the consent of their parents. He cannot marry such strangers as have bound themselves to serve a certain number of years, in order to pay off their passage from *Europe*, without the consent of their masters; if he acts without their consent, or in opposition to it, he must pay a penalty of fifty pounds, *Pensylvania* currency, though he has the licence, and the certificate of the two men who are to answer for any objection. But parents or masters give themselves no concern about these men, but take hold of the clergyman, who is at liberty to prosecute those who gave him the certificate, and to get his damages repaid. With the consent of the parents and masters he may marry people without danger to himself. No clergyman is allowed to marry a Negro with one of *European* extraction, or he must pay a penalty of one hundred pounds, according to the laws of *Pensylvania*.

NOTES

[1] Henry Melchior Mühlenberg (1711–1787) was educated in the Lutheran ministry at the University of Göttingen. He accepted a call from Philadelphia and came to America in 1742. Peter Brunnholz joined him in 1745. Mühlenberg's work was of crucial importance for the early organization of American Lutheranism.

4

Michel-Guillaume Jean de Crèvecoeur

Michel-Guillaume Jean de Crèvecoeur (1735–1813) has achieved
a secure place in the study of American civilization as the first
to articulate the question, What then is the American? which
so aptly represents that search for a national identity which still
claims our thoughtful attention two centuries later. Crèvecoeur
was born in Normandy and served under Montcalm in the
French and Indian wars. In 1765 he became an American citizen
and four years later settled with an American wife on his farm
in Orange County, New York, where he remained until his
return to France in 1780. During this period he wrote the
Letters from an American Farmer, one of the most thoughtful
and informative descriptions of eighteenth-century colonial life.
Like many thinkers of the century, he was an environmental
determinist. Humanity, stunted by corrupt, congested European
society, would flourish in that of America, which was free and
open. One of the important aspects of America's luxuriant social
climate was religion, here characterized, in Crèvecoeur's opinion, by freedom, toleration, and a salutary indifference.

[*from* LETTERS FROM AN AMERICAN FARMER]

WHAT attachment can a poor European emigrant have for
a country where he had nothing? The knowledge of the language, the love of a few kindred as poor as himself, were the

27

only cords that tied him: his country is now that which gives him land, bread, protection, and consequence: *Ubi panis ibi patria* is the motto of all emigrants. What then is the American, this new man? He is either an European, or the descendant of an European, hence that strange mixture of blood, which you will find in no other country. I could point out to you a family whose grandfather was an Englishman, whose wife was Dutch, whose son married a French woman, and whose present four sons have now four wives of different nations. *He* is an American, who leaving behind him all his ancient prejudices and manners, receives new ones from the new mode of life he has embraced, the new government he obeys, and the new rank he holds. He becomes an American by being received in the broad lap of our great *Alma Mater*. Here individuals of all nations are melted into a new race of men, whose labours and posterity will one day cause great changes in the world. Americans are the western pilgrims, who are carrying along with them that great mass of arts, sciences, vigour, and industry which began long since in the east; they will finish the great circle. The Americans were once scattered all over Europe; here they are incorporated into one of the finest systems of population which has ever appeared, and which will hereafter become distinct by the power of the different climates they inhabit. The American ought therefore to love this country much better than that wherein either he or his forefathers were born. Here the rewards of his industry follow with equal steps the progress of his labour; his labour is founded on the basis of nature, *self-interest*; can it want a stronger allurement? Wives and children, who before in vain demanded of him a morsel of bread, now, fat and frolicsome, gladly help their father to clear those fields whence exuberant crops are to arise to feed and to clothe them all; without any part being claimed, either by a despotic prince, a rich abbot, or a mighty Lord. Here religion demands but little of him; a small voluntary salary to the minister, and gratitude to God; can he refuse these? The American is a new man, who acts upon new principles; he must therefore entertain new ideas, and form new opinions. From involuntary idleness, servile dependence, penury, and useless labour, he has passed to toils of a very different nature, rewarded by ample subsistence. This is an American.

British America is divided into many provinces, forming a large association, scattered along a coast 1500 miles extent and about 200 wide. This society I would fain examine, at least such as it appears in the middle provinces; if it does not afford that variety of tinges and gradations which may be observed in Europe, we have colours peculiar to ourselves. For instance, it is natural to conceive that those who live near the sea must be very different from those who live in the woods; the intermediate space will afford a separate and distinct class.

Men are like plants; the goodness and flavour of the fruit proceeds from the peculiar soil and and exposition in which they grow. We are nothing but what we derive from the air we breathe, the climate we inhabit, the government we obey, the system of religion we profess, and the nature of our employment. Here you will find but few crimes; these have acquired as yet no root among us. I wish I were able to trace all my ideas; if my ignorance prevents me from describing them properly, I hope I shall be able to delineate a few of the outlines, which are all I propose.

Those who live near the sea feed more on fish than on flesh, and often encounter that boisterous element. This renders them more bold and enterprising; this leads them to neglect the confined occupations of the land. They see and converse with a variety of people; their intercourse with mankind becomes extensive. The sea inspires them with a love of traffic, a desire of transporting produce from one place to another; and leads them to a variety of resources which supply the place of labour. Those who inhabit the middle settlements, by far the most numerous, must be very different; the simple cultivation of the earth purifies them, but the indulgences of the government, the soft remonstrances of religion, the rank of independent freeholders, must necessarily inspire them with sentiments very little known in Europe among people of the same class. What do I say? Europe has no such class of men; the early knowledge they acquire, the early bargains they make, give them a great degree of sagacity. As freemen they will be litigious; pride and obstinacy are often the cause of law suits; the nature of our laws and governments may be another. As citizens it is easy to imagine that they will carefully read the newspapers, enter into every political disquisition, freely blame or censure governors and others. As farmers they will be careful and anxious to get as much as they can, because what they get is their own. As northern men they will love the chearful cup. As Christians, religion curbs them not in their opinions; the general indulgence leaves every one to think for themselves in spiritual matters; the laws inspect our actions, our thoughts are left to God. Industry, good living, selfishness, litigiousness, country politics, the pride of freemen, religious indifference, are their characteristics. If you recede still farther from the sea, you will come into more modern settlements; they exhibit the same strong lineaments, in a ruder appearance. Religion seems to have still less influence, and their manners are less improved. . . .

As I have endeavoured to shew you how Europeans become Americans; it may not be disagreeable to shew you likewise how the various Christian sects introduced, wear out, and how religious indifference becomes prevalent. When any considerable number of a particular sect happen to dwell contiguous to each other, they immediately erect a temple, and there worship the Divinity agreeably to their own peculiar ideas. Nobody disturbs them. If an new sect springs up in Europe, it may happen that many of its professors will come and settle in America. As they bring their zeal with them, they are at liberty to make proselytes if they can, and to build a meeting and to follow the dictates of their consciences; for neither the government nor any other power interferes. If they are peaceable subjects, and are industrious, what is it to their neighbours how and in what manner they think fit to address their prayers to the Supreme Being? But if the sectaries are not settled close together, if they are mixed with other denominations, their zeal will cool for want of fuel, and will be extinguished in a little time. Then the Americans become as to religion what they are as to country, allied to all. In them the name of Englishman, Frenchman, and European is lost, and in like manner, the strict modes of Christianity as practised in Europe are lost also. This effect will extend itself still farther hereafter, and though this may appear to you as a strange idea, yet it is a very true one. I shall be able perhaps hereafter to explain myself better, in the meanwhile, let the following example serve as my first justification.

Let us suppose you and I to be travelling; we observe that in this house, to the right, lives a Catholic, who prays to God as he has been taught, and believes in transubstantion; he works and raises wheat, he has a large family of children, all hale and robust; his belief, his prayers offend nobody. About one mile farther on the same road, his next neighbour may be a good honest plodding German Lutheran, who addresses himself to the same God, the God of all, agreeably to the modes he has been educated in, and believes in consubstantiation; by so doing he scandalizes nobody; he also works in his fields, embellishes the earth, clears swamps, &c. What has the world to do with his Lutheran principles? He persecutes nobody, and nobody persecutes him, he visits his neighbours, and his neighbours visit him. Next to him lives a seceder, the most enthusiastic of all sectaries; his zeal is hot and fiery, but separated as he is from others of the same complexion, he has no congregation of his own to resort to, where he might cabal and mingle religious pride with worldly obstinacy. He likewise raises good crops, his house is handsomely painted, his orchard is one of the fairest in the neighbourhood. How does it concern the welfare of the country, or of the province at large, what this man's religious sentiments are, or really whether he has any at all? He is a good farmer, he is a sober, peaceable, good citizen: William Penn himself would not wish for more. This is the visible character, the invisible one is only guessed at, and is nobody's business. Next again lives a Low Dutchman, who implicitly believes the rules laid down by the synod of Dort. He conceives no other idea of a clergyman than that of an hired man; if he does

his work well he will pay him the stipulated sum; if not he will
dismiss him, and do without his sermons, and let his church be
shut up for years. But notwithstanding this coarse idea, you will
find his house and farm to be the neatest in all the country; and
you will judge by his waggon and fat horses, that he thinks more
of the affairs of this world than of those of the next. He is sober
and laborious, therefore he is all he ought to be as to the affairs
of this life; as for those of the next, he must trust to the great
Creator. Each of these people instruct their children as well as
they can, but these instructions are feeble compared to those
which are given to the youth of the poorest class in Europe. Their
children will therefore grow up less zealous and more indifferent
in matters of religion than their parents. The foolish vanity, or
rather the fury of making Proselytes, is unknown here; they have
no time, the seasons call for all their attention, and thus in a few
years, this mixed neighbourhood will exhibit a strange religious
medley, that will be neither pure Catholicism nor pure Calvinism.
A very perceptible indifference even in the first generation, will
become apparent; and it may happen that the daughter of the
Catholic will marry the son of the seceder, and settle by themselves at a distance from their parents. What religious education
will they give their children? A very imperfect one. If there
happens to be in the neighbourhood any place of worship, we
will suppose a Quaker's meeting; rather than not shew their fine
clothes, they will go to it, and some of them may perhaps attach
themselves to that society. Others will remain in a perfect state
of indifference; the children of the zealous parents will not be
able to tell what their religious principles are, and their grand-
children still less. The neighbourhood of a place of worship
generally leads them to it, and the action of going thither is the
strongest evidence they can give of their attachment to any sect.
The Quakers are the only people who retain a fondness for their
own mode of worship; for be they ever so far separated from
each other, they hold a sort of communion with the society, and
seldom depart from its rules, at least in this country. Thus all
sects are mixed as well as all nations; thus religious indifference

is imperceptibly disseminated from one end of the continent to the other; which is at present one of the strongest characteristics of the Americans. Where this will reach no one can tell; perhaps it may leave a vacuum fit to receive other systems. Persecution, religious pride, the love of contradiction, are the food of what the world commonly calls religion. These motives have ceased here: zeal in Europe is confined; here it evaporates in the great distance it has to travel; there it is a grain of powder inclosed, here it burns away in the open air, and consumes without effect.

5

Thomas Coke

Thomas Coke (1747–1814) was the first Protestant bishop in America and the first Methodist to bear the title of bishop. He spent only a small portion of his lifetime in America, however, and is most appropriately associated with the English Wesleyan movement. Educated at Jesus College, Oxford, he entered the Anglican priesthood in 1772 but soon came under the Methodist influence. After losing his parish in 1776, he became one of Wesley's chief lieutenants and in 1784 was sent to America as a "superintendent," to exercise what were in effect *episcopal* powers. Though Wesley had preferred not to use the latter term, Coke preferred otherwise and in 1787 persuaded the American conference to change his title to bishop. This move not only touched off the first schism in American Methodism but outraged the founder of the movement as well. Wesley responded with words which still must amuse some of his followers: "Men may call me a knave or a foll, a rascal, a scoundrel, and I am content: but they shall never, by my consent, call me bishop."[1] Coke made nine visits to America between 1784 and 1803, but after Wesley's death, in 1791, his chief interest was English Methodism. The following is taken from the first American edition of his *Life of the Rev. John Wesley* (Philadelphia: John Dickins, 1793) and is valuable for its perspective on America's ecclesiastical history and its account of the circumstances which required Wesley's acquiescence in the formation of an autonomous Methodist denomination in America.

[*from* THE LIFE OF THE REV. JOHN WESLEY]

I N 1606, *James* the First erected two companies for the col-
onization of *New England*, then included under the general name
of *Virginia*. But no regular settlements were then formed: a
small trade only was carried on with the Indians. But under the
violent persecutions of the Non-conformists by Archbishop *Laud*,
many of that oppressed people fled for refuge to *New England*,
and with indefatigable and unremitted zeal, through almost every
difficulty and danger that could obstruct so hazardous an under-
taking, changed the face of a great tract of country from a waste
wilderness to an improved and cultivated land. These first Settlers, or very many of them at least, did undoubtedly experience
the vital power of godliness, and were joined by a multitude of
others, that fled from the tyranny of *Charles* the Second.

For some considerable time all the holy fruits of religion were
manifested among them. But, as usual, an uninterrupted flow of
prosperity damped the sacred flame: and perhaps their wars with
the Indian nations might also contribute towards it. Then
appeared the same spirit among themselves, which they had so
much opposed in *England*. The views of mankind were not
sufficiently enlarged at that period, to enable them to see the
importance of Universal Toleration to the prosperity of Society.
None of them seem to have had a conception that a most perfect
civil amity may be preserved among those who differ in the
speculative points of Theology. They therefore persecuted all
the emigrants, who, like themselves, had left their native country
for a more comfortable habitation than they found at home, but
who unhappily differed from them either in modes of worship
or religious sentiments. Of these the Quakers were the most
offensive to them, and were cruelly, yea, inhumanely treated by
them. Mercy and pure religion, inseparable companions, then
forsook the land. They lost their piety: and, to say the best of
them, were a *flourishing, commercial people*. . . .

In 1739, Mr. *George Whitefield* made his second visit to

America; and the Spirit of the Most High did indeed rest upon that great man. He revived that pure religion, which was so remarkable in the time of Dr. *Edwards*, but after his death had decayed. Great was his zeal, and great his success. "The Lord gave the word, and great was the company of the Preachers." The zealous Ministers raised by his labours, who were distinguished by the denomination of *New Lights*, became the most numerous body in *New England*: and, strange as it may appear, the old, wise, literary body of Presbyterians, in a synod held among themselves, formally thrust out or excommunicated *the majority*; declaring they would have no ministerial union with such an illiterate body of men. But the *real* Ministers of God were not to be silenced by such means. However, this revival also was but of short duration. Formality on the one hand, and Antinomianism on the other, again recovered their ascendency.

The States of *New York* and *New Jersey*, the former of which was first settled by the *English* in 1664, and the latter sometime in the reign of *Charles* II, were never remarkable for religion, till they were visited by some of the members of Mr. *Wesley's* Societies. Being so near *New England*, they indeed partook in a small measure of its revivals, especially those under Dr. *Edwards*[2] and Mr. *Whitefield*.

Pennsylvania, which formerly included the little state of *Delaware*, was possessed originally by the *Dutch* and *Swedes*; but was settled by the *English* in the reign of *Charles* II, under the direction of that great and good man, *William Penn*, the Quaker. The first settlers, as we may naturally expect, were chiefly persons of his own persuasion: and the Quakers make now a very considerable part of that State. They certainly had, and now have, real religion among them. The quaintness of their manners, and their ideas concerning the superior light of their dispensation, have kept them from being much known, and from being very useful. But the noble sacrifice of *all their slaves*, whom they have emancipated *to a man*, is a proof to a demonstration that the major part of the chief rulers of their Society at least, are devoted to the glory of God and the good of their neighbor.

In respect to the religion of *Pennsylvania* (that of the Quakers excepted) we can say but little in its commendation: though we doubt not but Mr. *Whitefield* kindled the flame of divine love in the hearts of several individuals, during his short visits to *Philadelphia*. So great a light must have shone in every place; and the power of the Holy Ghost which continually attended his Ministry, could not any where be entirely lost.

The five States to the South of those already mentioned, viz. *Maryland*, *Virginia*, *North* and *South Carolina*, and *Georgia*, may be considered together. The Baptists who are numerous in some parts of these States, have been useful to thousands both of whites and blacks. The abilities of their ministers in general were peculiarly small: but their zeal was much, and God was pleased to own it. To this day a considerable measure of real religion is to be found among them, though we fear that much of "the fine gold is become dross." A considerable number of their Preachers have embraced the doctrine of Universal Restitution, and thereby introduced much controversy and dissention into their church. Here and there, in that vast tract of country, from the most eastern point of *Maryland* to the most western point of *Georgia*, some ministers were also to be found, that sprung from the labours of Mr. *Whitefield*, who were more or less zealous for the salvation of souls.

But what shall we say for the Clergy of the Church of *England* in these States, at the time now under consideration? We would fain draw a veil over them, if the truth of history would permit it. Notwithstanding the purity and many other excellencies of their liturgy, articles and homilies, they were, with a few exceptions to the contrary, as bad a set of men as perhaps ever disgraced the Church of God: nor had their wretched flocks, at the distance of three or four thousand miles from the source of ecclesiastical power, the least hopes of redress. But we must acknowledge, and bless God for it, that the change has been abundantly for the better, since they have been favoured with an episcopacy of their own.

Such was the state of religion on that continent when the

present revival, by the means of Mr. *Wesley* and the Preachers in connection with him, was carried by divine Providence over the *Atlantic* ocean, and pierced through the immense forests of *America*. . . .

When the Civil War became general in that country, Mr. R.[3] with other Preachers from *England*, who had spoken publicly in behalf of the British Cause, were obliged to fly for their lives. And of all the *European* Missionaries, Mr. *Francis Asbury*[4] alone was determined to bear the heat and burden of that day.

Many of the Preachers, that were dubious concerning the merit of the war, and therefore scrupled to take the oaths of allegiance to the States in which they respectively laboured, were fined or imprisoned. But in every instance, those who were confined soon found some powerful friend, yea, often one who had no connection with the Society, who used his influence with the Governor and Council of the State, and obtained their liberty. Frequent instances there were, when the Preachers were brought before the Judges, that they bore such a pointed testimony against sin, and preached with such power the doctrines of the Gospel, that the Judges were at a loss in what manner to behave to them. Mr. *M.* a Preacher in *Baltimore*, delivered, on one of those occasions, such a sermon from the Bar, as filled the Judges and the whole Court with admiration, at the elegance of his diction, and the strength of his arguments. The Assembly of *Maryland*, partly perhaps to deliver the Judges from the trouble which was given them, and partly out of a spirit of candour, passed an Act expressly to allow the Methodist Preachers, so called, to exercise their function without taking the oath of allegiance.

During the Civil War, the societies were destitute of the sacraments, except in two or three of the cities. They could not obtain baptism for their children, or the Lord's supper for themselves, from the Presbyterian, Independent, or Baptist Ministers, but on condition that they would leave the society of which they were members, and join those churches respectively: and many of the clergy of the Church of *England* had left the country. The societies in general were so grieved on this account, and so influenced the minds of the Preachers by their incessant complaints, that in the year 1778, a considerable number of them earnestly importuned Mr. *Asbury* to take proper measures, that the people might enjoy the privileges of all other churches, and no longer be deprived of the christian sacraments. Mr. *Asbury's* attachment to the church of *England* was at that time exceeding strong: he therefore refused them any redress. On this *the majority* of the Preachers withdrew from him, and consequently from Mr. *Wesley*, and chose out of themselves three senior brethren who ordained others by the imposition of their hands. The Preachers thus set apart, administered the sacraments to those they judged proper to receive them, in every place where they came. However Mr. *Asbury*, by indefatigable labour and attention, and by all the address in his power, brought them back one after another: and by a vote of one of the Conferences, the Ordination was declared invalid; and a perfect reunion took place.

When peace was established between *Great Britain* and the *States*, the intercourse was opened betwixt the societies in both countries. Mr. *Wesley* then received from Mr. *Asbury* a full account of the progress of the work during the war; and especially of the division which had taken place, and the difficulties he met with, before it was healed. He also informed Mr. *Wesley* of the extreme uneasiness of the people's minds for want of the sacraments: that thousands of their children were unbaptized, and the members of the societies in general had not partaken of the Lord's supper for many years. Mr. *Wesley* then considered the subject, and informed Dr. *Coke* of his design of drawing up a plan of Church-government, and of establishing an Ordination for his *American* societies. But, cautious of entering on so new a plan, he afterwards suspended the execution of his purpose, and weighed the whole for upwards of a year.

At the Conference held in *Leeds*, 1784, he declared his intention of sending Dr. *Coke* and some other Preachers to *America*. Mr. *Richard Whatcoat* and Mr. *Thomas Vasey* offered themselves as Missionaries for that purpose, and were accepted. Before they sailed, Mr. *Wesley* abridged the Common Prayer-book of the Church of *England*, and wrote to Dr. *Coke*, then in *London*, desiring him to meet him in *Bristol*, to receive fuller powers; and to bring the Rev. Mr. *Creighton* with him. The Dr. and Mr. *Creighton* accordingly met him in *Bristol*; when, with their assistance, he ordained Mr. *Richard Whatcoat* and Mr. *Thomas Vasey* Presbyters for *America*: and, did afterwards ordain Dr. *Coke* a Superintendent, giving him Letters of Ordination under his hand and seal, and at the same time a letter to be printed, and circulated in *America*, of which the following is an extract.[5]

Bristol, Sept. 10, 1784.

To Dr. Coke, Mr. Asbury, and our Brethren in North-America.

"By a very uncommon train of providences, many of the provinces of *North-America* are totally disjoined from their mother-country, and erected into independent States. The *English* government has no authority over them either civil or ecclesiastical, any more than over the States of *Holland*. A civil authority is exercised over them, partly by the Congress, partly by the provincial Assemblies. But no one either exercises or claims any ecclesiastical authority at all. In this peculiar situation some thousands of the inhabitants of these States desire my advice; and in compliance with their desire, I have drawn up a little sketch.

"For many years I have been importuned from time to time, to exercise the right of ordaining part of our travelling Preachers. But I have still refused: not only for peace' sake; but because I was determined as little as possible to violate the established order of the national Church to which I belonged.

"But the case is widely different between *England* and *North-America*. Here there are Bishops who have a legal jurisdiction. In *America* there are none, neither any parish Ministers. So that for some hundred miles together there is none either to baptize or to administer the Lord's supper. Here therefore my scruples are at an end: and I conceive myself at full liberty, as I violate no order, and invade no man's right, by appointing and sending labourers into the harvest.

"I have accordingly appointed Dr. *Coke* and Mr. *Francis Asbury*, to be joint *Superintendents* over our brethren in *North-America*: as also *Richard Whatcoat* and *Thomas Vasey*, to act as *Elders* among them, by baptizing and administering the Lord's supper. And I also advise the Elders to administer the supper of the Lord on every Lord's day.

"If any one will point out a more rational and scriptural way of feeding and guiding those poor sheep in the wilderness, I will gladly embrace it. At present I cannot see any better method than that I have taken.

"It has indeed been proposed, to desire the *English* Bishops to ordain part of our Preachers for *America*. But to this I object, 1. I desired the Bishop of *London* to ordain only one; but could not prevail. 2. If they consented, we know the slowness of their proceedings; but the matter admits of no delay. 3. If they would ordain them *now*, they would likewise expect to govern them. And how grievously would this entangle us? 4. As our *American* brethren are now totally disentangled both from the State and from the *English* Hierarchy, we dare not entangle them again, either with the one or the other. They are now at full liberty, simply to follow the Scriptures and the Primitive Church. And we judge it best that they should stand fast in that Liberty, wherewith God has so strangely made them free.

John Wesley."

NOTES

[1] John Wesley to Francis Asbury in John Telford (ed.), *The Letters of the Rev. John Wesley* (London: The Epworth Press, 1931), Vol. VIII, pp. 90–91.

[2] Jonathan Edwards (1703–1758), theologian, philosopher and Congregational minister, was one of the most powerful thinkers America has produced. He led the defense of Calvinist orthodoxy in the early eighteenth century. His efforts to revive an ardent piety in his Northampton congregation culminated in an extensive revival in 1734 and 1735 and paved the way for Whitefield's success a few years later.

3 Thomas Rankin (d. 1810) was sent to America by John Wesley in 1773 to supervise the work of the Methodist societies here. He returned to England in 1778.

4 Francis Asbury (1745–1816) was sent by Wesley as a missionary to American Methodists in 1771. He was the only English Methodist leader to remain during the revolution. He was elevated to the episcopacy with Coke in 1784, and the prosperity of Methodism in the early national period was due largely to his heroic efforts.

5 Wesley, Coke, and James Creighton had all been ordained presbyters in the Church of England. Wesley had long believed that a presbyter had the same powers as a bishop, including the power of ordination. Yet he had not exercised this power until circumstances in America compelled him to do so. On September 2, 1784, Wesley and Creighton ordained Richard Whatcoat and Thomas Vasey as elders (presbyters) and Thomas Coke as "superintendent," the title Coke later changed to bishop. Coke, Vasey, and Whatcoat then came to America, where, at the Christmas Conference of that year, American Methodism was organized as an autonomous religious body.

6

William Cobbett

William Cobbett (1762–1835) was one of the most colorful
figures in English history. Of peasant birth and entirely self-
educated, he rose through military service and a lifetime of
political journalism to become one of the leading English
radicals of the nineteenth century, ending his career with a seat
in the first reform Parliament. On two occasions he made extended visits to America. Becoming embroiled in a legal battle
after his army service was completed, he fled to France and
from there to Philadelphia, where from 1792 to 1800 he was
known as an outspoken Federalist and Anglophile. His political
preferences underwent a change when he returned, however,
and after 1804 he was increasingly identified with the English
reform movement. Fearing imprisonment when the Habeas
Corpus Act was suspended, he fled to America again in 1817
and remained this time for two years. An account of his second
visit was published in 1818 as *Journal of a Year's Residence in
the United States of America*. In that work, from which the
following excerpt is taken, Cobbett used his description of
things American to promote his political objectives in England,
making it in part an Englishman's assessment of America, in part
a chapter in English reform polemics.

[*from* JOURNAL OF A YEAR'S RESIDENCE IN
THE UNITED STATES OF AMERICA]

TAXES *and Priests*; for these always lay on heavily together.
On the subject of taxes, I have, perhaps, spoken sufficiently clear
before; but, it is a great subject. I will, on these subjects, address

myself more immediately to *my old neighbours of Botley*, and endeavour to make them understand what America is as to taxes and priests. . . .

I have talked to several farmers here about the tithes in England; and, they *laugh*. They sometimes almost make me angry; for they seem, at last, not to believe what I say, when I tell them that the English farmer gives, and is compelled to give, the Parson a tenth part of his whole crop and of his fruit and milk and eggs and calves and lambs and pigs and wool and honey. They cannot believe this. They treat it as a sort of *romance*. . . .

But, my Botley neighbours, you will exclaim, "No *tithes*! Why, then, there can be no *Churches* and no *Parsons*! The people must know nothing of God or Devil; and must all go to hell!" By no means, my friends. Here are plenty of Churches. No less than three Episcopal (or English) Churches; three Presbyterian Churches; three Lutheran Churches; one or two Quaker Meeting-houses; and two Methodist Places; all within *six miles* of the spot where I am sitting. And, these, mind, not poor shabby Churches; but each of them larger and better built and far handsomer than Botley Church, with the Church-yards all kept in the neatest order, with a head-stone to almost every grave. As to the Quaker Meeting-house, it would take Botley Church into its belly, if you were first to knock off the steeple.

Oh, no! Tithes are not necessary to promote *religion*. When our Parsons, such as Baker, talk about *religion*, or *the church*, being in danger; they mean that the *tithes* are in danger. They mean that they are in danger of being compelled to work for their bread. This is what they mean. You remember that, at our last meeting at Winchester, they proposed for us to tell the Prince Regent that we would *support the Church*. I moved to leave out the word *church*, and insert the word *tithes*; for, as there were many presbyterians and other dissenters present, they could not, with clear consciences, pledge themselves to support *the church*. This made them *furious*. It was lifting up the *mask*; and the parsons were enraged beyond measure.

Oh, no! *Tithes* do not mean *religion*. Religion means *a rever-*

ence for God. And, what has this to do with tithes? Why cannot you reverence God without Baker and his wife and children eating up a tenth part of the corn and milk and eggs and lambs and pigs and calves that are produced in Botley parish? The Parsons, in this country, are supported by those who choose to employ them. A man belongs to what congregation he pleases. He pays what is required by the rules of the congregation. And, if he thinks that it is not necessary for him to belong to any congregation, he pays nothing at all. And, the consequence is, that all is harmony and good neighborhood. Here are not disputes about religion; or, if there be, they make no noise. Here is no ill-will on this account. A man is never asked what religion he is of, or whether he be of any religion at all. It is a matter that nobody interferes in. What need, therefore, is there of an *established* Church. What need is there of tithes? And, why should not that species of property be taken for *public use?* That is to say, as far as it has any thing to do with religion? I know very well, that tithes do not operate as many people pretend; I know that those who complain most about them have the least right to complain; but, for my present purpose, it is sufficient to shew, that they have nothing to do with *religion.*

If, indeed, the Americans were wicked, disorderly, criminal people, and, of course, a miserable and foolish people: then we might doubt upon the subject: then we might possibly suppose that their wickedness and misery arose, in some degree, at least, from the *want of tithes*. But, the contrary is the fact. They are the most orderly, sensible, and least criminal people in the whole world. A common labouring man has the feelings of a man of honour; he never thinks of violating the laws; he crawls to nobody; he will call every man *Sir*, but he will call no man *master*. When he utters words of respect towards any one, they do not proceed from fear or hope, but from civility and sincerity. A native American labourer is never *rude* towards his employer, but he is never *cringing*. . . .

In short, blindfold an Englishman and convey him to New York, unbind his eyes, and he will think himself in an English city. The same sort of streets; shops precisely the same; the same beautiful and modest women crowding in and out of them; the same play-houses; the same men, same dress, same language: he will miss by day only the nobility and the beggars, and by night only the street-walkers and pickpockets. These are to be found only where there is an *established* clergy, upheld by what is called the *state*, and which word means, in England, the Borough-mongers.

Away, then, my friends, with all cant about *the church*, and the church being in danger. If the church, that is to say, the *tithes*, were completely *abolished*; if they, and all the immense property of the church, were taken and applied to public use, there would not be a sermon or a prayer the less. Not only the Bible but the very Prayer-book is in use here as much as in England, and, I believe, a great deal *more*. Why give the five millions a year then, to Parsons and their wives and children? Since the English, Irish, and Scotch, are so good, so religious, and so moral here without glebes and tithes; why not use these glebes and tithes for other purposes, seeing they are possessions which can legally be disposed of in another manner?

But, the fact is, that it is the circumstance of the church *being established by law* that makes it *of little* use as to real religion, and as to morals, as far as they be connected with religion. Because, as we shall presently see, this establishment forces upon the people, parsons whom they cannot respect, and whom indeed, they must *despise*; and, it is easy to conceive that the moral precepts of those, whom we despise on account of their immorality, we shall never much attend to, even supposing the precepts themselves to be good. If a precept be self-evidently good; if it be an obvious duty which the parson inculcates, the inculcation is useless to us, because, whenever it is wanted to guide us, it will occur without the suggestion of any one; and, if the precept be not self-evidently good, we shall never receive it as such from the lips of a man whose character and life tell us we ought to suspect the truth of every thing he utters. When the matters as to which we are receiving instructions are, in their nature, wholly dissimilar to those as to which we have witnessed the conduct of the teacher, we may reasonably, in listening to the precept, disregard that conduct. Because, for instance, a man, though a very indifferent Christian, may be a most able soldier, seaman, physician, lawyer, or almost any thing else; and what is more, may be honest and zealous in the discharge of his duty in any of these several capacities. But, when the conduct, which we have observed in the teacher belongs to the same department of life as the precept which he is delivering, if the one differ from the other we cannot believe the teacher to be sincere, unless he, while he enforces his precept upon us, acknowledge his own misconduct. Suppose me, for instance, to be a great liar, as great a liar, if possible, as STEWART of the COURIER, who has said that I have been "fined 700 dollars for writing against the American government," though I never was prosecuted in America in all my life. Suppose me to be as great a liar as STEWART, and I were to be told by a parson, whom I knew to be as great a liar as myself, that I should certainly go to hell if I did not leave off lying. Would his words have any effect upon me? No: because I should conclude that if he thought what he said, he would not be such a liar himself. I should rely upon the parson generally, or I should not. If I did, I should think myself safe until I out-lied him; and, if I did not rely on him generally, of what use would he be to me?

Thus, then, if men be *sincere* about religion; if it be not all a mere matter of form, it must always be of the greatest consequence that the example of the teacher correspond with his teaching. And the most likely way to insure this, is to manage things so that he may in the first place, be selected by the people, and, in the second place, have no rewards in view other than those which are to be given in consequence of his perseverance in a line of good conduct.

And thus it is with the clergy in America, who are duly and amply rewarded for their diligence, and very justly respected for the piety, talent, and zeal which they discover; but, who have no tenure of their places other than that of the will of the congregation. Hence it rarely indeed happens, that there is seen amongst them an impious, an immoral, or a despicable man. Whether the teaching of even these Reverend parsons have any very great effect in producing virtue and happiness amongst men is a question upon which men may, without deserving to be burnt alive, take the liberty to differ; especially since the world has constantly before its eyes a society who excel in all the Christian virtues, who practise that simplicity which others teach, who, in the great work of charity, really and truly hide from the left hand that which the right hand doeth; and who know nothing of Bishop, Priest, Deacon, or Teacher of any description. Yes, since we have the Quakers constantly before our eyes, we may, without deserving to be burnt alive, question the utility of paying any parsons or religious teachers at all.

7

Achille Murat

In its early years the United States often sheltered European royalty and nobles who were escaping from revolutionary republicans and other enemies at home. One of those sheltered was Achille Murat (1801–1847), the eldest son of Joachim Murat, whom Napoleon had made king of Naples in 1808. Achille Murat spent his boyhood as a crown prince, but when Joachim was overthrown he fled with his mother to Trieste and then to Vienna. Austria, however, held few opportunities for Bonapartists after 1815, and in 1823 Murat came to the United States, where he spent the rest of his life. He settled in Florida, near Tallahassee, bought a plantation, took an American wife and began to practice law. He published a series of letters in France; these letters were the basis of his *Esquisse morale et politique des Etats-Unis de l'Amérique du Nord* (1832). In this work he proclaimed his love of republican institutions and expressed especial pleasure with the state of religion in America, since it presaged the imminent collapse of Christianity altogether.

[*from* A MORAL AND POLITICAL SKETCH]

WHILE a death-struggle is waging in Europe between those who would maintain institutions, the offspring of ages of barbarism, and those who would raise them to a level with modern enlightenment; while in every civilized part of the globe, a more or less considerable portion of every nation is agitated with a desire for a state of liberty, which they do not know, and which they

49

seek more from instinct than calculation, marching towards that great end by fallacious paths, which only lead them further from it; it is curious to observe the tranquillity which prevails in the United States, the only country in the world in which the principles of liberty are established without mixture or opposition. It is a government something similar to this which is now called for by the wishes of all the nations of Europe; but owing to their ignorance of the object of their desires, their efforts are almost always ill directed. These reflections are suggested to me by the popular tumults which have lately taken place in France, during which the people amused themselves by pulling down crosses from churches; and by the law which assimilates the rabbins to the catholic priests and protestant ministers, in making them pensioners of the State. It is not for me to criticize or to approve what has been done in France; I shall content myself with giving you a sketch of the state of religion in the United States, where it exists free and independent of the government without being at all in each other's way. You will easily gather, from what I am about to tell you, my own opinions on this subject.

Do not suppose however that I am going to undertake an exposition of all the dogmas of the thousand and one sects which divide the people of the United States. Merely to enumerate them would be impossible, for they change every day, appear, disappear, unite, separate, and evince nothing stable but their instability. From the pure doctrines of Unitarianism to the gross absurdities of Methodism, all shades may be found here, and every opinion has its partisans, who live in perfect harmony together. Among this variety of religions, everybody may indulge his inclination, change it whenever he pleases, or remain neuter, and follow none. Yet, with all this liberty, there is no country in which the people are so religious as in the United States; to the eyes of a foreigner they even appear to be too much so; but that is only apparent, as I shall explain to you.

When the States of New England were first peopled by persons banished from the mother-country on account of religion, they established among themselves a species of theocratic government. Although the persecutions they had suffered ought to have taught them tolerance, they began to persecute with all their might Quakers, catholics, and witches. They had digested a code of laws called, I know not why, "blue laws," which established a variety of ridiculous practices as an integral part of good morals. The Sunday was to be observed in the most rigorous manner; on that day people were not permitted either to travel or to walk in the streets (except to and from church), nor to cook, nor even to kiss their wives. A particular cut was prescribed for the hair, and certain dishes allowed only at particular times of the year. A thirty-sixth of the public lands were set apart in each town to endow a school and a church, of any denomination whatever, provided it were Protestant. In the States colonized by government, such as Virginia and South Carolina, the Church of England was established as in the mother-country, and so it remained until the revolution. The Catholics, banished from England, founded Maryland, and then introduced intolerance. Louisiana and the Floridas, settled by French and Spaniards, had churches and convents richly endowed. It was reserved to the great Penn to be the first to establish unlimited toleration in the colony of Pennsylvania. This system was gradually followed by the other colonies, and is now the law in all the States. On the adoption of the constitution of the United States, the principle of general toleration was not only adopted as part of the federal compact, but Congress was even interdicted from legislating upon religion. In all the States, the churches and their property, if they have any, belongs not to the ministers, but to the congregations. Thus, when a new city is founded, a lot is put aside for the first congregation which may demand it; trustees are appointed, to whom and to their successors in office the lands are given or sold for the use of such or such congregation. From that moment the corporation is formed, and becomes a person empowered to *bargain and sell, to sue and be sued*, according to the conditions prescribed by the charter of incorporation. This body corporate collects gifts, borrows money, builds a church, sells part of the pews, lets others, sells or lets choice places in the churchyard, &c.; and when all this is done, elects a pastor, pays him, keeps him, dismisses him, changes him, as it pleases. Sometimes a minister has a fixed salary only, sometimes only fees, besides the use of a house or the rent of the pews. In short, each congregation makes its agreement with its pastor, as it chooses. Many of these congregations are very rich, many are poor, or, wasting their means, become bankrupt, in which case, their church is sold by auction, like any other property. It often happens that a preacher is thought to preach some doctrine ill-sounding to pious ears. The bishop or the consistory excommunicate him; in which case, the congregation either changes its religion and keeps its pastor, or changes its pastor and keeps its religion. It generally happens, that the excommunicated pastor, with a minority of the congregation, form a new sect; then a new corporation is formed, and a new church built or bought. The sect takes, and other churches of the same denomination are established; or it dies with its founder, and the congregation either again changes its religion, or is divided, or remains without a pastor; which last, however, is not very common. . . .

All these congregations, conventions, &c. are only recognized by the law as corporations, having the faculty of buying, selling, sueing and being sued at law, in the same manner as other corporations whose object is charity, public works, or commercial speculations. Masonic lodges and chapters are incorporated in the same manner, as well as museums, picture galleries, and learned societies. The privileges of the clergy are limited to being exempt from militia duty, and from serving on the jury, the same as postmasters, schoolmasters, doctors, &c. In some States also they are exempt from paying tolls at bridges and gates, when travelling for religious purposes; in some others, they are ineligible to all public employments. But these privileges and these disqualifications apply equally to the ministers of all religions, provided they are recognized as such by a congregation, and do not continue if they quit the church. Everybody, indeed, who has the desire, may preach if he can find auditors (a matter of no difficulty); and from that moment he becomes a clergyman. . . .

The great number of religious societies existing in the United States is truly surprising: there are some of them for every thing; for instance, societies to distribute the Bible, to distribute tracts, to encourage religious journals, to convert, civilize, educate the savages; to marry the preachers, to take care of their widows and orphans; to preach, extend, purify, preserve, reform the faith; to build chapels, endow congregations, support seminaries, catechise and convert sailors, Negroes, and loose women; to secure the observance of Sunday, and prevent blasphemy, by prosecuting the violators; to establish Sunday schools, where young ladies teach reading and the catechism to little rogues, male and female; to prevent drunkenness, &c.

This last society in particular is very singular, and very much extended. The members engage never to drink any distilled liquor, nor to permit its use in their families; but nothing hinders them from drinking wine. In that they mistake the Creator for a bad chemist. The number of these societies is always increasing by hundreds, because there is forthwith one at least of each sort in each State, and for each sect or denomination. Thus there are Protestant-episcopal, Methodist-episcopal, Methodist, Presbyterian, Baptist, Evangelical, &c., Tract Societies for the State of New York, New Jersey, Pennsylvania, &c.&c. There is no end to them. Of course, whatever may be the object of the society, there must be at least a secretary and a treasurer, an office, office charges, printing, postage, clerks, and all the appointments of a public office, all which are filled by preachers, and more or less remunerated. This explains a little how it is that the vineyard of the Lord is so flourishing; it is by these means that immense sums are extracted from the pockets of the people. There is certainly no clergy so costly to the people as the American clergy; but it is only fair to add that these contributions are strictly voluntary, and I, for instance, have no right to complain, for no preacher ever received a cent from me.

But that you may see their proceedings in all their lustre, transport yourself to the end of Nassau Street, in New York; there you will see a magnificent building, with white marble steps and front: it belongs to a Bible Society, as the gold letters above indicate. Go in: a long corridor gives access to numerous rooms with mahogany doors; read the inscriptions on these doors: "office of such or such society"; "office of the Reverend Mr. Such-a-one, treasurer or secretary of such or such society." Proceed further, you will find a great bloated reverend gentleman perched upon a three-foot stool before a desk, busy in posting his ledger; around him some junior reverends assist him in his labour. You are, to all intents and purposes, in a counting-house. I know it, because I have had drafts upon these gentlemen; and all the difference I have found between them and a banker has been that they always invited me to give up the change to them, for the purposes of the society.

A young man, therefore, who enters into the church, always finds his place, and the means of making, if not a fortune, at least of drawing from thence a pleasant existence amidst abundance. If he be good-looking, he marries; if a man of talent, he preaches, becomes the head of a sect, and writes; if he have an aptitude for business, he invents some new society, takes upon himself the direction of its affairs, and look about you as sharply as you please, you will be cheated.

You will ask me, probably, after reading this, if religion, supported by such means, and disposing of such capitals, does not make great progress, and if it does not bid fair soon to penetrate everything? On the contrary; with difficulty does it keep its footing; it is like a ship sailing against the tide, which seems to make much way if we look at the water, and remains stationary in respect to the shore; in the same way is the church carried away by the great current of opinions, literature, and modern philosophy, which nothing can resist. This, above all, is the great opposing power, and which will certainly end by overthrowing the Christian religion; perhaps even this overthrow, considered as that of a complete system, is more advanced in the United States than is generally believed. But, besides that, other causes conspire to the same effect; the rising influence of the Unitarian sect is, perhaps, one of the most powerful. Pure theists, en-lightened and virtuous philosophers, they do not, it is true, openly attack superstition, but they take away the support of their names, which is much. Boston, for instance, was the centre of bigotry; it is become that of this philosophic sect, and the chief seat of letters. Every distinguished man in that city, whether in politics or literature, is an Unitarian. The University of Cambridge, which is near by, is the head quarters of the sect, and it spreads from one end of the Union to the other. But, in addition to this, there are other philosophic sects which make a direct war on religion. . . .

It must be admitted that looking at the phisiognomy of the United States, its religion is the only feature which disgusts a foreigner. A Sunday, particularly in the north and east, is a day of gloom, and calculated to make one regret any other sojourn, even exile in Vienna. The Israelites in the desert longed for the fleshpots of Egypt. On that day there is no theatre, no visiting; the shops are shut, the streets deserted, the communications interrupted. The post office of the United States is barely permitted to send despatches, and this, thanks to the southern representatives. People go out only to go to church. Every body wears a sullen and taciturn air. Families have no cooking on that day; they live on the leavings of the day before. The women assemble in a circle, each with a Bible in hand, which she makes believe to read while yawning. The men do the like, or under that pretext shut themselves up on their closet and look into their private business, sure of not being interrupted on the sabbath, as it is called. But, who do they mean to deceive? I often said to myself, when looking on similar scenes, and knowing the individual opinions of the different members. The fact is that nobody is deceived, although there is a desire to deceive every body. Every body knows very well the degree of sincerity there is in the religion of his neighbour, but nobody likes to be the first to take off the mask. The master is there, every body is a candidate for his favour in a country in which public opinion reigns without mixture. He must be flattered, and the flatterers deceive themselves as to his opinions. The notion generally entertained of the strength of religious prejudices is much exaggerated, and the time is not far distant which will terminate the influence of the clergy and the forced hypocrisy which it produces, and show that those who willingly submit to it constitute a very feeble minority. The sceptical party has only to know its strength, to shake off entirely the yoke of superstition, and for some time it has been making immense progress towards that object. The influence of the clergy, moreover, is merely apparent; it is absolute, certainly, upon matters of form, but at bottom nobody cares for it. Even formerly it was not strong enough to hinder the election of Mr. Jefferson, who denied publicly all belief in the Bible. Now it could do still less: in fifty years it will be able to do nothing.

8

Auguste Levasseur

In 1824 the renowned Lafayette, hero of the American and French revolutions, accepted the invitation of President Monroe to make a fourth visit to the United States. Lafayette was nearing seventy years of age, and though he was yet to play an important role in the July Revolution of 1830, his American visit was assumed to be his final appearance here and thus the last opportunity to show honor and respect for one of the greatest men of the century. From August 1824 to June 1825 Lafayette traveled through all the states of the Union, honored guest at a year-long series of solemn patriotic occasions. He was accompanied by his son, his valet, and his secretary, Auguste Levasseur. Levasseur had been an officer in the French army, associated with one of the revolutionary military societies supported by Lafayette (perhaps the *Charbonnerie*), and had recently resigned his commission to become a member of Lafayette's household staff. Most of Levasseur's book is filled with solemn tributes and notable personages, but he did find time and space for some of his own observations of American life. As a French republican and heir of Voltaire's anticlericalism, he was most impressed with the manner in which American patriotism was infused with religious sentiment.

[*from* LAFAYETTE IN AMERICA]

THE people of Connecticut rigidly observe religious practices; but they have long been free of that spirit of persecution which animated the founders of the colony, whose first ecclesiastical ordinance, in taking possession of the soil in 1637, denied the rights of citizenship to all those who would not entirely and without reserve, submit to the forms of the established religion. At the present time, when religious liberty is sanctioned by law, reciprocal tolerance of different communions has established a sort of fraternity among them. We had a striking evidence of it during the Sabbath we spent in New London. On arriving in that city, General Lafayette, that he might not in any thing offend the habits of that excellent people, from whom he was receiving such touching expressions of affection, had expressed a desire to be present at divine worship. Immediately the Congregationalists and the Episcopalians, who compose the principal communions of the place, offered him places in their churches. It was difficult to accept the offer of one without disobliging the other; and the General sent them word that he would cheerfully attend both. This reply spread great joy in the city. We first went to the Congregational church, and afterwards to the Episcopal: we found them both surrounded and filled with a crowd without distinction of sects; in both, the sermons included morality, without the discussion of peculiar doctrines, and ended with eulogiums on *him whom God had so many times conducted through the dangers of the ocean, to secure the happiness and liberty of America*. These sermons were listened to with equal attention by all. On leaving church the two ministers cordially shook hands with each other, felicitating themselves at the pleasure of having had the guest of the nation among them. . . .

The extreme severity of character which distinguished the first inhabitants of New England has been gradually effaced by contact with other nations, and above all by the introduction of toleration in religious opinions. The rigour of the puritans has given place to an agreeable harmony between the numerous sects which divide among themselves not only New England, but the whole Union. It is not however to be concluded that zeal has given away to indifference. Religious practices are observed with scrupulous exactness. It would be difficult to find in Boston a party devoted to amusement on the Sabbath. The chains which were formerly stretched before the churches during the celebration of solemn services, have by degrees disappeared. The government is not permitted to interfere in any manner in religious concerns; the pastors of the different churches are paid by their parishioners. If in public particular respect is shown for those who frequent the churches, no one ever pretends to persecute those who never make their appearance in them. Finally, there remains not more than a single trace of the religious tyranny of the first colonists; and this trace is unfortunately found in the constitution. The first article of the sixth chapter excludes from the offices of the government every candidate who does not belong to the Christian religion, and who does not swear that he is convinced of its truth. "I, A.B. do declare, that I believe the Christian Religion, and have a firm persuasion of its truth." . . .

The college of Columbia, founded some time ago, as yet contains only a very small number of students The choice of the directors and professors promises something brilliant hereafter; but the college at Georgetown is a powerful rival. That establishment, which we visited the day after our arrival at Washington, and in which General Lafayette was received with every testimony of gratitude and patriotism, is under the direction of the Jesuits. When I saw the *Reverends* in the costume of their order, I could not at first suppress a painful sentiment. All the misdeeds of which they have been guilty in Europe crowded up in my imagination; and I lamented the blindness of the Americans who trust the education of their children to a sect so inimical to liberty. On my return to Washington, I could not forbear communicating my fears to Mr. Cambreleng,[1] a young representative from New York, in whose company I spent the evening. He at first listened with a smile; but when he heard me express a wish that all Jesuits were rigorously excluded from giving public education, he shook his head in disapprobation. "That measure," said he, "will never be adopted among us: at least, I hope not. In my opinion, it would be contrary to that spirit of liberty which animates us; it would be unjust towards the Jesuits, of whom we never had any ground for complaint; and besides, I know no power in our country which possesses authority to take such a measure." "It is possible," replied I, "that you may have no ground for complaint against the Jesuits, because they are as yet very few among you, and have not arrived at power; but have a little patience, think what has happened in Europe, and tremble." "What has happened in Europe," replied he, "can never happen among us, because we are wise enough not to change our institutions: while we have neither *king*, nor *state religion*; nor *monopoly*, we never can have to fear either the intrigues or the influence of any *association*. With whom could the Jesuits intrigue here?—the Government? With us the government is the people. I can easily conceive how in Europe the Jesuits may gain the ear of the king by means of intrigues, and by filling his mind with religious fears; by means of which, they draw from him wealth, honour, power, &c. But can you believe sincerely, that, with all their intrigue and address you suppose them to possess, your Jesuits can ever succeed in persuading a whole nation, enlightened and free, to spoil themselves, and deliver themselves up, bound hand and foot? Never! Besides, by what means would they persuade them?" "By means of public instruction," replied I. "But," returned he, "before public instruction could become the effectual means of operation to them, it must be monopolized by them. Now! thanks to our wise institutions, we have no monopolies of any kind. We do not groan like you, under the leaden weight of a privileged University. Among us, every father of a family is the only judge of the manner in which it is proper to educate and instruct his children; and hence arises a concurrence between those who devote themselves to public instruction: a concurrence which sustains itself only by a sincere attachment to our institutions, a profound respect for the laws we have made for ourselves, and the practice of all virtues which compose the character of good citizens. The Jesuits themselves are obliged to fulfil these conditions, in order to obtain the confidence of the public; and they thus obtain it, so long as they merit it. I do not see by what authority they can be deprived of the exercise of a right which is common to us all; and if they should ever show themselves unworthy, the public would do them justice." "Ah!

indeed," replied I, "among us also, public opinion would do them justice; but public opinion cannot expel them from the University, nor from the king's council, nor from the wealthy establishments they have founded, nor from the offices they have obtained." "Very well," coolly replied my young representative; *get rid of all these things*, and your Jesuits will then be no more dangerous than our own." . . .

General Lafayette, who, while he well appreciates the unfortunate position of slave-holders in the United States, and cannot overlook the greater part of the obstacles which oppose an immediate emancipation of the blacks, still never fails to take advantage of an opportunity to defend the right which *all men, without exception*, have to liberty, introduced the question of slavery among the friends of Mr. Madison. It was approached and discussed by them with frankness, and in such a manner as to confirm the opinion I had before formed of the noble sentiments of the greater part of the Virginians on that deplorable subject. It seems to me that slavery cannot subsist much longer in Virginia: for the principle is condemned by all enlightened men; and when public opinion condemns a principle, its consequences cannot long continue.

After the question of corporeal slavery in the United States, they referred to the no less important questions of the mental slavery, to which some of the nations of Europe are condemned by the prevailing religions: the religions of the state. The friends of Mr. Madison congratulated themselves that at least this species of slavery is unknown in the United States; and they entered into certain particulars, from which I learned that they were not the kind of men to be easily contented with what we always speak of in Europe as a benefit: I mean religious *tolerance*. "Tolerance," said one of them, "is doubtless preferable to persecution; but it would be insupportable in a free country, because it is marked by an insulting pride. Before the right of tolerating is conceded to any sect or religion, and before the others are reduced to suffer the shame of being *tolerated*, it must first be proved that only one is good, and the others bad. But how is this proof to be obtained, while every body believes his own to be the best? The word *tolerance* is therefore an insult, and can be reasonably substituted only by the word *liberty*. Religious liberty we possess in the full extent of its meaning; and may assert, that there is not one out of all our twenty-four states in which it is not better understood than in any part of Europe. We, however, have had our periods of tolerance, I will even say of intolerance. Before our glorious revolution, for example, we groaned under the laws by which, for certain degrees of heresy, a father might forfeit the right of educating his children, and his claim to the protection of certain laws, and even be burnt. Now, how great is the difference! Thanks to our new laws, worthy of the immortal legislators who were entrusted with framing them, no individual can be compelled to practice any religious worship, nor to frequent any place, nor to support any minister, of any religion whatever; nor constrained, restrained, disturbed or oppressed in his person or property; and finally, none can be persecuted in any manner on account of religious opinions: but all men have liberty to *profess, and sustain by argument*, their opinions in matters of religion, and those opinions cannot diminish, increase or produce any thing in respect to their civil rights."

I had lent an attentive ear, as may well be supposed, to this interesting conversation; and one of those who had taken part in the conversation, and had observed it, took me aside, while Mrs. Madison was preparing tea, and said: "Since you feel so lively an interest in all that relates to our excellent institutions, I will communicate to you a fact to which my friend has not referred, doubtless through fear of offending the modesty of the master of the house. You may perhaps know that, before the revolution, the English church was dominant in this state; and its ministers, discontented with the equality in different sects established by the law of 1776, and still more by the law of 1779, which deprived them of the appointments they had received from the government, declared that they should not be content with voluntary contributions for their support, and laid a petition before the General Assembly, during the sessions of 1784 and 1785, for securing *the support of ministers of the gospel* by the government. That petition, although supported by the most popular talents in the house, seemed likely to receive a majority of votes, when, to prevent its success, several members requested and obtained its postponement to the succeeding session, and had it printed, that it might be submitted to the public opinion. During that time, Colonel G. Mason and Colonel G. Nicholas requested Mr. Madison to draw up an argument against the petition, which was extensively distributed among the people, and with such success, that it soon received a prodigious number of signatures from men of all sects and communions, and in the following session, the petition was rejected with decision.[2] You would, I have no doubt, be gratified with a perusal of that document, which, in my opinion, contains the wisest and strongest arguments that can be used in favour of religious liberty; and I can send you one to-morrow, as I still possess several copies.

"Since the declaration of religious liberty which stood its ground against that petition, there has not been any national religion in the United States. The expenses of public worship are defrayed by voluntary contributions. This state of things singularly contrasts with the policy of European nations; and yet religion is not neglected among us. It is true that the people in the country have not many places where they can perform religious worship; but it is to be remembered that they are scattered in small numbers, over a new territory; and that Europe owes the magnificence of her churches, not to the religious zeal of an enlightened period, but to the superstition and bigotry of an ignorant age. Besides, it will be remarked, that in the great cities of Europe, where the excess of population does not correspond with the ancient funds of the church, the edifices for religious worship are still more disproportionate to the numbers of the people than in the United States. In 1817, Boston, with a population of 40,000, contained twenty-three churches; New York, whose inhabitants amounted to 120,000, contained fifty-three; and Philadelphia, with 100,000 inhabitants, had forty-eight; Cincinnati, in the state of Ohio, containing 8000 inhabitants, although at that time it had been founded scarcely seven years, contained five churches, and two others were building. A comparison can be drawn only between the great cities; and if the support of churches be regarded as a decisive proof of zeal for religion, we are to remark that new churches are built in Europe by taxes, while in the United States they are raised by means of voluntary contributions."

On the following morning, before we left Montpellier, I accordingly received the document alluded to, which I perused with interest, and found it deserving of the eulogium which had been bestowed upon it. The principles it inculcates are so simple and so eloquently maintained and defended that it seems to me difficult to add any thing new on the subject. . . .

In these repeated recitals which I have made of public exhibition that I witnessed, during my visit to the United States, one must be struck at the constant union of religious ideas with patriotic sentiments, which so strongly characterize the citizens of that republic; but what is no less worthy of remark is that their religion, freed from minute ceremonies, resembles a sentiment, as much as their love of liberty resembles a creed. Among them a political orator never closes a preparatory address without invoking or returning thanks to the Almighty; as a minister, when he ascends the pulpit, always begins by reminding his audience of their duties as citizens, and the happiness they enjoy in living under wise institutions. It may be said that this mixture of political morality and theology extends through all the actions of the Americans, a tincture of gravity and profound conviction, the charm and influence of which I cannot express. Thus, for example, how can the following simple and affecting invocation, from the Rev. William Latta, be heard without producing a deep feeling, and drawing out our gratitude to mingle with his? We were about to take our seats at a dinner, given to the guest of the nation by the citizens of West Chester, when the president of the day, remarking that a minister of the gospel was among the number of guests, and that he requested him to ask a blessing, the Rev. William Latta immediately pronounced a benediction to which he added these words:

"Almighty God, our Heavenly Father! we render thee thanks

for the benefits which thou hast bestowed upon the American people and the memory of which we celebrate this day. We give thee thanks that thou didst pour into the minds of our fathers the pure love of freedom, and didst inspire the heart of the stranger whom we this day welcome among us with the desire to adopt our cause and our dangers; that, amidst all the dangers to which he has been exposed thou hast preserved his life precious, to enable him, after half a century, to revisit our country, to receive the expression of the people's thanks, and to see the fruits of that independence which he so powerfully contributed to establish."

A committee from the town of Lancaster had come to seek General Lafayette at Chester, which place we left on the 27th, after bidding farewell to a great number of soldiers of 1776, who could not take leave of their old General for the last time without shedding tears.

I think I have already mentioned the remarkable fact that, in the north and the south, we had seen men of different habits and languages, controlled, for their common advantage, by the same democratic government, and living in harmony in the midst of private happiness and public prosperity, under the aegis of the same institutions. From this observation we are naturally led to conclude that neither the greatness of a state, nor the difference in the habits of the inhabitants of its territory, are obstacles to the establishment and operation of a republican government which is founded on an equal appreciation of the interests of all. Perhaps nothing was more likely to confirm General Lafayette in this opinion than the sight of Lancaster, and the county of that name, where is found a complete collection of men from all parts of America and Europe, almost all of different religious creeds, but all equally attached to the wise institutions by which they are governed.

NOTES

[1] Churchill Caldom Cambreleng (1786–1862) was a member of Congress from 1821 to 1839 and served as House administrative leader for Jackson and Van Buren.

[2] The text of the "Memorial and Remonstrance against Religious Assessments" can be found in Saul Padover (ed.), *The Complete Madison* (New York: Harper & Brothers, 1953), pp. 299–306.

9

Frances Trollope

Probably no foreign visitor was better known or more heartily disliked by nineteenth-century Americans than Mrs. Frances Trollope (1780–1863). She was a quick-witted, outspoken woman who found much in the United States which displeased her. Mrs. Trollope's stay in America was the result of domestic misfortunes. Her husband had failed as a lawyer and a farmer in England and hoped to recover his losses by investing what remained of his money in a bazaar for the sale of fancy merchandise in Cincinnati. The Trollopes lived in America from 1827 until their return to England in 1831, after the failure of the Cincinnati enterprise. Mrs. Trollope's book *The Domestic Manners of the Americans*, written just before her return and published early in 1832, launched her at the age of fifty-two on a literary career which soon brought her a measure of financial security. She found more than enough social and theological evils in the American voluntary system to reinforce her loyalty to the Church of England.

[*from* THE DOMESTIC MANNERS OF THE AMERICANS]

I NEVER saw any people who appeared to live so much without amusement as the Cincinnatians. Billiards are forbidden by law, so are cards. To sell a pack of cards in Ohio subjects the seller to a penalty of fifty dollars. They have no public balls, excepting, I think, six, during the Christmas holidays. They have no concerts. They have no dinner parties.

They have a theatre, which is, in fact, the only public amusement of this triste little town; but they seem to care little about it, and either from economy or distaste, it is very poorly attended. Ladies are rarely seen there, and by far the larger proportion of females deem it an offence against religion to witness the representation of a play. It is in the churches and chapels of the town that the ladies are to be seen in full costume: and I am tempted to believe that a stranger from the continent of Europe would be inclined, on first reconnoitering the city, to suppose that the places of worship were the theatres and cafes of the place. No evening in the week but brings throngs of the young and beautiful to the chapels and meeting-houses, all dressed with care, and sometimes with great pretension; it is there that all display is made, and all fashionable distinction sought. The proportion of gentlemen attending these evening meetings is very small, but often, as might as expected, a sprinkling of smart young clerks make this sedulous display of ribbons and ringlets intelligible and natural. Were it not for the churches, indeed, I think there might be a general bonfire of best bonnets, for I never could discover any other use for them.

The ladies are too actively employed in the interior of their houses to permit much parading in full dress for morning visits. There are no public gardens or lounging shops of fashionable resort, and were it not for public worship, and private tea-drinkings, all the ladies in Cincinnati would be in danger of becoming perfect recluses.

The influence which the ministers of all the innumerable religious sects throughout America have on the females of their respective congregations approaches very nearly to what we read of in Spain, or in other strictly Roman Catholic countries. There are many causes for this peculiar influence. Where equality of rank is affectedly acknowledged by the rich, and clamorously claimed by the poor, distinction and pre-eminence are allowed to the clergy only. This gives them high importance in the eyes of the ladies. I think, also, that it is from the clergy only that the women of America receive that sort of attention which is so dearly valued by every female heart throughout the world. With the priests of America the women hold that degree of influential importance which, in the countries of Europe, is allowed them throughout all orders and ranks of society, except, perhaps, the very lowest; and in return for this they seem to give their hearts and souls into their keeping. I never saw, or read, of any country where religion had so strong a hold upon the women, or a slighter hold upon the men.

I mean not to assert that I met with no men of sincerely religious feelings, or with no women of no religious feelings at all; but I feel perfectly secure of being correct as to the great majority in the statement I have made. . . .

I had often heard it observed, before I visited America, that one of the great blessings of its constitution was the absence of a national religion, the country being thus exonerated from all obligation of supporting the clergy; those only contributing to do so whose principles led them to it. My residence in the country has shown me that a religious tyranny may be exerted very effectually without the aid of the government, in a way much more oppressive than the paying of tithe, and without obtaining any of the salutary decorum which I presume no one will deny is the result of an established mode of worship.

As it was impossible to remain many weeks in the country without being struck with the strange anomalies produced by its religious system, my early notes contain many observations on the subject; but as nearly the same scenes recurred in every part of the country, I state them here, not as belonging to the west alone, but to the whole Union, the same cause producing the same effect every where.

The whole people appear to be divided into an almost endless variety of religious factions, and I was told that to be well received in society, it was necessary to declare yourself as belonging to some one of these. Let your acknowledged belief be what it may, you are said to be *not a Christian* unless you attach yourself to a particular congregation. Besides the broad and well-known distinctions of Episcopalian, Roman Catholic, Presbyterian, Calvinist, Baptist, Quaker, Swedenborgian, Universalist, Dunker,

&c.&c. &c., there are innumerable others springing out of these, each of which assumes a church government of its own; of this, the most intriguing and factious individual is invariably the head; and in order, as it should seem, to show a reason for this separation, each congregation invests itself with some queer variety of external observance that has the melancholy effect of exposing *all* religious ceremonies to contempt.

It is impossible, in witnessing all these unseemly vagaries, not to recognise the advantages of an established church as a sort of headquarters for quiet unpresuming Christians, who are contented to serve faithfully, without insisting upon having each a little separate banner, embroidered with a device of their own imagining.

The Roman Catholics alone appear exempt from the fury of division and sub-division that has seized every other persuasion. Having the Pope for their common head, regulates, I presume, their movements, and prevents the outrageous display of individual whim, which every other sect is permitted.

I had the pleasure of being introduced to the Roman Catholic bishop of Cincinnati,[1] and have never known in any country a priest of a character and bearing more truly apostolic. He was an American, but I should never have discovered it from his pronunciation or manner. He received his education partly in England, and partly in France. His manners were highly polished; his piety active and sincere, and infinitely more mild and tolerant than that of the factious Sectarians who form the great majority of the American priesthood.

I believe I am sufficiently tolerant; but this does not prevent my seeing that the object of all religious observances is better obtained when the government of the church is confided to the wisdom and experience of the most venerated among the people than when it is placed in the hands of every tinker and tailor who chooses to claim a share in it. Nor is this the only evil attending the want of a national religion, supported by the State. As there is no legal and fixed provision for the clergy, it is hardly surprising that their services are confined to those who can pay them.

The vehement expressions of insane or hypocritical zeal, such as were exhibited during "the Revival," can but ill atone for the want of village worship, any more than the eternal talk of the admirable and unequalled government can atone for the continual contempt of social order. Church and State hobble along, side by side, notwithstanding their boasted independence. Almost every man you meet will tell you that he is occupied in labours most abundant for the good of his country; and almost every woman will tell you that besides those things that are within (her house), she has coming upon her daily the care of all the churches. Yet spite of this universal attention to the government, its laws are half asleep; and spite of the old women and their Dorcas societies, atheism is awake and thriving.

In the smaller cities and towns, prayer-meetings take the place of almost all other amusements; but as the thinly-scattered population of most villages can give no parties, and pay no priests, they contrive to marry, christen, and bury, without them. A stranger taking up his residence in any city in America must think the natives the most religious people upon earth; but if chance lead him among her western villages, he will rarely find either churches or chapels, prayer or preacher; except, indeed, at that most terrific saturnalia, "a camp-meeting." I was much struck with the answer of a poor woman, whom I saw ironing on a Sunday. "Do you make no difference in your occupations on a Sunday?" I said. "I beant a Christian, Ma'am; we have got no opportunity," was the reply. It occurred to me, that in a country where "all men are equal," the government would be guilty of no great crime, did it so far interfere as to give them all *an opportunity* of becoming Christians if they wished it. But should the federal government dare to propose building a church, and endowing it, in some village that has never heard "the bringing home of bell and burial," it is perfectly certain that not only the sovereign state where such an abomination was proposed would rush into the Congress to resent the odious interference, but that all the other states would join the clamour, and such an intermeddling administration would run great risk of impeachment and degradation.[2]

Where there is a church government so constituted as to deserve human respect, I believe it will always be found to receive it, even from those who may not assent to the dogma of its creed; and where such respect exists, it produces a decorum in manners and language often found wanting where it does not. Sectarians will not venture to rhapsodise, nor infidels to scoff, in the common intercourse of society. Both are injurious to the cause of rational religion, and to check both must be advantageous.

It is certainly possible that some of the fanciful variations upon the ancient creeds of the Christian Church, with which transatlantic religionists amuse themselves, might inspire morbid imaginations in Europe as well as in America; but before they can disturb the solemn harmony *here*, they must prelude by a defiance, not only to common sense, but what is infinitely more appalling, to common usage. They must at once rank themselves with the low and the illiterate, for only such prefer the eloquence of the tub to that of the pulpit. The aristocracy must ever, as a body, belong to the established Church, and it is but a small proportion of the influential classes who would be willing to allow that they do not belong to the aristocracy. That such feelings influence the professions of men, it were ignorance or hypocrisy to deny; and that nation is wise who knows how to turn even such feelings into a wholesome stream of popular influence. . . .

If any one chooses to say that some wicked antipathy to twelve millions of strangers is the origin of my opinion, I must bear it; and were the question one of mere idle speculation, I certainly would not court the abuse I must meet for stating it. But it is not so. I know that among the best, the most pious, the most benevolent of my countrymen, there are hundreds, nay, I fear thousands, who conscientiously believe that a greater degree of political and religious liberty (such as is possessed in America) would be beneficial for us. How often have I wished, during my abode in the United States, that one of these conscientious, but mistaken reasoners, fully possessed of his country's confidence, could pass a few years in the United States, sufficiently among the mass of the citizens to know them, and sufficiently at leisure to trace effects to their causes. Then might we look for a statement which would teach these mistaken philanthropists to tremble at every symptom of democratic power among us; a statement which would make even our sectarians shudder at the thought of hewing down the Established Church, for they would be taught, by fearful example, to know that it was the bulwark which protects us from the gloomy horrors of fanatic superstition on one side, and the still more dreadful inroads of infidelity on the other. And more than all, such a man would see as clear as light that where every class is occupied in getting money, and no class in spending it, there will neither be leisure for worshipping the theory of honesty, nor motive strong enough to put its restrictive doctrines in practice. Where every man is engaged in driving hard bargains with his fellows, where is the honoured class to be found, into which gentlemanlike feelings, principles, and practice, are necessary as an introduction?

NOTES

[1] Rev. Edward Fenwick (1768–1832) was bishop of the Cincinnati Diocese from 1822 until his death.

[2] Several observers saw the provision of religious facilities in the western settlements as the crucial test of the voluntary system. For contrasting opinions on this matter see Francis Grund, p. 78 and Andrew Reed, pp. 100–2.

IO

Francis Grund

Francis Grund (1798–1863) has not yet received the recognition he deserves as one of the most perceptive European commentators on America in the nineteenth century. His *Aristocracy in America* was republished in 1959, but *The Americans in Their Moral, Social, and Political Relations*, which is a much more comprehensive statement of his reflections on America has not been reprinted since 1837. Grund was born in Austria and educated at the University of Vienna; in 1827 he emigrated to the United States, where he became an American citizen and spent an active career in political journalism. His books on America are grounded on much longer and more intimate experience of America than most European travelers had. Moreover, they contain the reflections of a thoughtful student of human society, one whose gaze was sympathetic, but never superficial. His remarks about the merging of Christian piety and American nationalism are a striking anticipation of recent sociological analyses and suggest that the origins of this phenomenon are to be found in the pre-Civil War era.

[*from* THE AMERICANS]

IF republicans are at all permitted to display splendour and magnificence without offending the pride of their fellow citizens, it is certainly in the edifices of public worship, and in the halls of their legislative assemblies. With regard to the latter, the Americans possess, already, a proud monument of national grandeur. The capitol at Washington, situated on an eminence commanding an unobstructed view of many miles in circumference, is an edifice of the most imposing structure and proportions; and, from its very position, incredibly superior to any of the public palaces in Europe. The interior, too, corresponds well with the dignity of the design: but the most sublime effect is produced by its standing high, free, and alone, as the institutions it guards in its bosom; overshadowing hills, and valleys, and rivers of the mighty land over which it exerts the benign influence of law and justice.

But proud as the Americans may be of their halls of congress, they have not, as yet, a single place of worship at all to be compared to the finer churches in Europe, where they might render thanks to the Omnipotent Being for the unexampled happiness and prosperity with which he has blessed their country. Some not altogether unsuccessful attempts have been made in Boston and Baltimore at what might be called a cathedral; but neither the size nor the order, nor even the materials, are resembling those of the nobler specimens of Gothic architecture in Europe.

Our feelings and emotions are always tinged with the reflections from the objects around us; and I cannot, therefore, divest myself of the opinion that a superior style of architecture in an edifice of public worship may materially assist the imagination, and enable the mind to turn from mere worldly objects to the contemplation of heaven and the adoration of God. I have known persons who could never pray so fervently as when encompassed by the sombre vaults of a Gothic cathedral, and I have, myself, experienced the same feelings on similar occasions.

But in addition to the deficiency in style and ornament, there exists, in America, an almost universal practice of building churches, or at least the steeples, of wood, to which are frequently given the most grotesque figures, partaking of all orders of architecture, from the time of Noah to the present day. There is scarce an excuse for this corruption of taste, except the cheapness of the material, which may recommend the custom in practice. A church ought to be the symbol of immutability and eternity, the attributes of the Infinite Being; but nothing can be more averse to either than its construction of so frail a material as wood. An *imitation* of stone-work is still more objectionable, as it appears like an attempt at deceit; a sort of architectural counterfeiting least pardonable in a house of prayer. Such an edifice seems to be unworthy of its noble purpose; a sordid mockery of grandeur which, without elevating the mind, represents to it only the melancholy picture of human frailties.

Yet the Americans are not deficient in liberality toward their clergymen, whose pecuniary compensation is certainly generous, when compared with the moderate salaries of the first officers of state, and enables them generally to live in houses much more tastefully built, and better furnished within, than those in which they deliver their sermons.

This is again republican, and shows the Americans to be much more attached to substance than to forms. The most essential part of divine service is assuredly performed by the clergyman, whose example and admonitions have a more salutary influence on the general morals of his congregation than the most gorgeous cathedral, or the most moving *cantabile* of Haydn. Yet the latter have their advantages too, which, no doubt, will, at some future day, be duly appreciated in America as in Europe. In the Western States, where new settlements are daily forming, it would be absurd to erect buildings the use of which would be reserved for the third or fourth generation. The principal object, there, must necessarily be immediate usefulness; and it is certainly better for the people to worship in a wooden church than to have no church at all.

Another cause operating against the erecting of costly churches in the United States is the absence of a powerful hierarchy. Churches in America are built when they are wanted, or whenever a congregation is sufficiently numerous and able to pay a preacher. With them the clergyman must be of more importance than the church, in the building of which they voluntarily tax themselves, without having recourse to the pecuniary assistance of others. This will always keep the church poor; but I doubt whether the practice, while it lasts, does not actually benefit the people; I am convinced there is as good preaching in the United States, and quite as fervent too, as in any country with a church-establishment.

Setting aside the injustice (of which Americans at least are fully persuaded) of taxing people of a different belief with the support of an establishment in which they have no stake or interest, there is in an hierarchy that which makes its members indolent and lazy. A person provided for cannot, by the rules of common sense, be supposed to work as hard as one who has to exert himself for a living, or whose services are remunerated in proportion to their merit and usefulness. An hierarchy, from its superior organisation and discipline, may have its *political* advantages under peculiar forms of government; but I cannot see any spiritual benefit accruing from it to the people. Every member of a hierarchy is necessarily more interested in *the continuance of the establishment* than in the discharge of his duties *toward the people*. He is paid by the establishment, of which he is either a functionary or a pensioner, and is as much concerned in its welfare as a British mariner in the safety and endurance of Greenwich Hospital, or a clerk in the solvency of his employers. In America, every clergyman may be said to do business on his own account, and under his own firm. He alone is responsible for any deficiency in the discharge of his office, as he is alone entitled to all the credit due to his exertions. He always acts as principal, and is therefore more anxious, and will make greater efforts to obtain popularity, than one who serves for wages. The actual stock in any one of those firms is, of course, less than the immense capital of the Church of England; but the aggregate amount of business transacted by them jointly may nevertheless be greater in the United States. The subordinate member of a hierarchy does not act on his own responsibility; he merely discharges the obligations enjoined by his superiors. It is to them he must look for advancement, as a soldier looks for promotion to his commanding officers; and a fault of discipline is more severely reprimanded than an actual injustice towards a different order. Like the soldier he has frequently an interest different from that of the people; and, like him, he is ready to turn his weapons against them whenever the establishment itself is in danger. A church establishment resembles always, more or less, a standing army. It is strong, endurable, and disciplined, but a severe tax upon the people, and nearly as dangerous an instrument for their subjugation.

The situation of an American clergyman is usually comfortable; but there are no church-livings as in England; no rich prelates or other high dignitaries sufficiently wealthy to employ large sums in the building of churches. Every preacher is paid by his congregation; and there is, consequently, no accumulation of wealth on the part of the clergymen, nor a proportionate poverty on the part of those who employ them. The conditions of the different members of the clergy are, as nearly as possible, on a level with each other and those of the private citizens; no distinction being claimed, save that which is based on superior talent and application. Hence the American churches resemble each other as the dwelling houses. They are built for use, but not for ornament; and are neither calculated to attract particular attention, nor to embellish or adorn the cities.

But what they lack in quality is more than compensated by increase of numbers; and in this consists the advantage of the system. There is no village in the United States without its church, no denomination of Christians in any city without its house of prayer, no congregation in any of the new settlements without the spiritual consolation of a pastor. Religious instruction is obtained, every where, at a comparatively cheap rate, without directly taxing the people; and the enormous sum which would be required for the maintenance of an established church circulates freely in commerce and manufactures, and contributes to the general prosperity of the country. . . .

The Americans consider their ministers as public servants, paid by their respective congregations in proportion to the degree of their usefulness. It is a principle with them to establish no sinecures, either in religion or politics; and their clergy, therefore, have less fortune and leisure to employ in their personal improvement *as gentlemen*, though they have ample time for the cultivation of that more substantial knowledge in a minister, which teaches him to imitate the example of his great Master; and, by winning the hearts of his congregation, and influencing their morals by his own irreproachable life, to become truly the pastor of his flock, and the friend and counsellor of every family in his parish. Such were the ministers of the pilgrims, and such, it is to be hoped, will be the ministers of the gospel in the United States yet for many a generation. And the people with a simplicity which does credit to both their hearts and their understandings, value these qualifications in their clergymen higher than the strongest claims of the latter to the refined tastes of gentlemen. . . .

When we reflect that no tax is imposed for the support of ministers, or the building of churches, and that consequently all those establishments are the result of voluntary contributions of the people; the conviction will certainly be forced on our minds that the Americans are deeply impressed with the importance of religious instruction, and that together with their freedom they prize nothing so high as the sacred truths of Christianity. No more satisfactory evidence is required on this subject than the fact that they are willing to *pay* for it; which is certainly a singular coincidence when contrasted with the political position of other countries. If there were an established religion of state, I doubt whether half the money could be raised for its support which is now cheerfully expended for the maintenance of twenty-five different doctrines.

The American ministers are continually striving to make proselytes, and, being usually paid in proportion to the number of communicants, anxious to increase the number of their respective congregations. I do not mean to say that this is the only motive of their religious ardour; but merely speak of the advantages of the system over all others, independent of the intrinsic merits of the ministers. The principle of paying most "where most work is done," or where it is done best, which is daily producing miracles in the United States, is even applicable to the clergy; and is productive of more good to mankind than could be produced with twice the funds in any country in Europe. Not only have the Americans a greater number of clergymen than, in proportion to the population, can be found either on the Continent or in England; but they have not one idler amongst them; all of them being obliged to exert themselves for the spiritual welfare of their respective congregations. The Americans, therefore, enjoy a threefold advantage: they have more preachers; they have more active preachers, and they have cheaper preachers than can be found in any part of Europe.

The religious habits of the Americans form not only the basis of their private and public morals, but have become so thoroughly interwoven with their whole course of legislation that it would be impossible to change them without affecting the very essence of their government. Not only are the manners and habits of a people, at all times, stronger than the positive law; but the latter itself is never readily obeyed without becoming reduced to a custom. It is to the manners and habits of a nation we must look for the continuance of their government. In France, where the people have for ages been accustomed to an absolute and despotic government, where every historical monument, every palace, every work of art, nay, the very furniture of their rooms, speak monarchy, we perceive constant anomalies in society, from the legislative halls down to the meanest public resort; simply because the people are accustomed to feel one way, and constrained to reason and act in another. They possess yet the forms of religion, which have ceased to convey to them a meaning; they have yet the splendour of a throne, without any of the feelings of loyalty; they have all the titles and pretensions of their ancient nobles, with the most unbounded love of equality. Yet with all their political excitability, and their theoretical attachment to republicanism, they are constantly lulled asleep by monarchical principles, without offering any other resistance than the sensation which the fact itself produces, when set off by the pen of an editor. An Englishman or an American would *feel* the encroachment on his liberty; because it would oblige him to change his habits, which he is less prepared to do than to surrender a positive right. American liberty is further advanced in the minds of the people than even in the laws themselves. It has become an active principle which lives with, and animates, the nation, and of which their political constitution is but a *facsimile*.

Whatever contributes to confirm a people in the habitual exercise of freedom is an additional guarantee of its continuance; and whatever has been instrumental in procuring that freedom, or is associated with it in their minds, must be preserved with religious care, lest liberty itself should suffer in their estimation. This is the case with the doctrines of Christianity in the United States. Religion has been the basis of the most important American settlements; religion kept their little community together, religion assisted them in their revolutionary struggle; it was religion to which they appealed in defending their rights, and it was religion, in fine, which taught them to *prize* their liberties. It is with the solemnities of religion that the declaration of independence is yet annually read to the people from the pulpit, or that Americans celebrate the anniversaries of the most important events in their history. It is to religion they have recourse whenever they wish to impress the popular feeling with anything relative to their country; and it is religion which assists them in all their national undertakings. The Americans look upon religion as a promoter of civil and political liberty; and have, therefore, transferred to it a large portion of the affection which they cherish for the institutions of their country. In other countries, where religion has become the instrument of oppression, it has been the policy of the liberal party to *diminish* its influence; but in America its promotion is essential to the constitution. Religion presides over their councils, aids in the execution of the laws, and adds to the dignity of the judges. Whatever is calculated to diminish its influence and practice, has a tendency to weaken the government, and is consequently opposed to the peace and welfare of the United States. It would have a direct tendency to lessen the respect for the law, to bring disorder into their public deliberations, and to retard the administration of justice.

The deference which the Americans pay to morality is scarcely inferior to their regard for the Christian religion, and is considered to be based upon the latter. The least solecism in the moral conduct of a man is attributed to his want of religion, and is visited upon him as such. It is not the offence itself; but the outrage on society, which is punished. They see in a breach of morals a direct violation of religion; and in this, an attempt to subvert the political institutions of the country. These sentiments are all-powerful in checking the appearance of vice, even if they are not always sufficient to prevent its existence. With Argus-eyes does public opinion watch over the words and actions of individuals; and whatever may be their private sins, enforces at least a tribute to morality in public.

My meaning cannot be misunderstood: It is but the open violation of the law which comes before the forum of the judge; for our secret transgressions we shall have to account with our God. Public virtue must be guarded against the pernicious influence of example; vice must be obliged to conceal itself, in order not to tincture society in general. In this consists the true force and wholesome influence of public opinion. It becomes a mighty police-agent of morality and religion, which not only discovers crimes; but prevents their commission. The whole people of the United States are empanelled as a permanent jury to pronounce their verdict of "guilty" or "not guilty" on the conduct and actions of men, from the President down to the labourer; and there is no appeal from their decision. Public opinion may sometimes be unjust for a long time, especially in reference to politicians; but it hardly ever remains so, and there is no injury which it inflicts which it is not in its power to remedy. . . .

Morality, in America, is not only required of a statesman; but is equally necessary in every occupation of life. The merchant who employs a clerk, the master-workman who employs a journeyman, the gentleman who hires a servant will all make morality an indispensable condition of contract. In this they are as much guided by their own choice as by the opinions of their neighbours and the community in general. An inferior workman of "steady habits" is almost always preferred to one possessed of the highest business qualifications, but with a doubtful moral character. Thus, a married man will be sooner trusted than one who is single; because "he has given hostage to fortune," and possesses what Bacon calls "an impediment to mischief." A man of sober habits will be sooner employed than one addicted to intemperance; and a clumsy, but moral servant will more readily obtain a situation than one who is expert and vicious. Religion will, in all, be considered as a pledge of morality; and a lax observance of religious duties, as a bad index to their private virtues. In short, morality and religion are as indispensable to the labouring classes in the United States as powerful and well-formed limbs and a correct use of the understanding. They will often atone for a variety of other imperfections; but without them every other qualification becomes useless, and only serves to aggravate the despair of success.

II

Alexis de Tocqueville

Alexis de Tocqueville (1805–1859) was sent to America by the French government in 1831 to report on the penal system in the United States. The most important result of his visit, however, was his *Democracy in America* (1835), a searching analysis of American institutions and social life by a careful student of politics. The aristocratic Tocqueville was by no means an ardent admirer of democracy but he sensed that it was the direction in which Europe was moving and wished to learn what he could about it in order to mitigate its effects in France. This attitude toward his subject combined with his ability to perceive American phenomena in the context of a thorough understanding of European institutions produced a classic study of American civilization. Like Levasseur, Tocqueville was surprised by the way in which the voluntary arrangements for religion had made possible an alliance of Christianity and democracy and had largely avoided the anticlericalism that characterized liberal politics in Europe.

[*from* DEMOCRACY IN AMERICA]

I THINK that the Catholic religion has erroneously been looked upon as the natural enemy of democracy. Among the various sects of Christians, Catholicism seems to me, on the contrary, to be one of those which are most favorable to the equality of conditions. In the Catholic Church, the religious community is composed of only two elements, the priest and the people. The priest alone rises above the rank of his flock, and all below him are equal.

On doctrinal points the Catholic faith places all human capacities upon the same level; it subjects the wise and ignorant, the man of genius and the vulgar crowd, to the details of the same creed; it imposes the same observances upon the rich and the needy, it inflicts the same austerities upon the strong and the weak, it listens to no compromise with mortal man, but, reducing all the human race to the same standard, it confounds all the distinctions of society at the foot of the same altar, even as they are confounded in the sight of God. If Catholicism predisposes the faithful to obedience, it certainly does not prepare them for inequality; but the contrary may be said of Protestantism, which generally tends to make men independent, more than to render them equal.

Catholicism is like an absolute monarchy; if the sovereign be removed, all the other classes of society are more equal than they are in republics. It has not infrequently occurred that the Catholic priest has left the service of the altar to mix with the governing powers of society, and to take his place among the civil gradations of men. This religious influence has sometimes been used to secure the interests of that political state of things to which he belonged. At other times Catholics have taken the side of aristocracy from a spirit of religion.

But no sooner is the priesthood entirely separated from the Government, as is the case in the United States, than it is found that no class of men are more naturally disposed than the Catholics to transfuse the doctrine of the equality of conditions into the political world. If, then, the Catholic citizens of the United States are not forcibly led by the nature of their tenets to adopt democratic and republican principles, at least they are not necessarily opposed to them; and their social position, as well as their limited number, obliges them to adopt these opinions. Most of the Catholics are poor, and they have no chance of taking a part in the Government unless it be open to all the citizens. They constitute a minority, and all rights must be respected in order to insure to them the free exercise of their own privileges. These two causes induce them, unconsciously, to adopt political doctrines which they would perhaps support with less zeal if they were rich and preponderant.

The Catholic clergy of the United States has never attempted to oppose this political tendency, but it seeks rather to justify its results. The priests in America have divided the intellectual world into two parts: in the one they place the doctrines of revealed religion, which command their assent; in the other they leave those truths which they believe to have been freely left open to the researches of political inquiry. Thus the Catholics of the United States are at the same time the most faithful believers and the most zealous citizens.

It may be asserted that in the United States no religious doctrine displays the slightest hostility to democratic and republican institutions. The clergy of all the different sects hold the same language, their opinions are consonant to the laws, and the human intellect flows onward in one sole current. . . .

The sects which exist in the United States are innumerable. They all differ in respect to the worship which is due from man to his Creator, but they all agree in respect to the duties which are due from man to man. Each sect adores the Deity in its own peculiar manner, but all the sects preach the same moral law in the name of God. If it be of the highest importance to man, as an individual, that his religion should be true, the case of society is not the same. Society has no future life to hope for or to fear; and provided the citizens profess a religion, the peculiar tenets of that religion are of very little importance to its interests. Moreover, almost all the sects of the United States are comprised within the great unity of Christianity, and Christian morality is everywhere the same.

It may be believed without unfairness that a certain number of Americans pursue a peculiar form of worship, from habit more than from conviction. In the United States the sovereign authority is religious, and consequently hypocrisy must be common; but there is no country in the whole world in which the Christian religion retains a greater influence over the souls of men than in America; and there can be no greater proof of its utility, and of its conformity to human nature, than that its influence is most powerfully felt over the most enlightened and free nation of the earth.

I have remarked that the members of the American clergy in general, without even excepting those who do not admit religious liberty, are all in favor of civil freedom; but they do not support any particular political system. They keep aloof from parties and from public affairs. In the United States religion exercises but little influence upon the laws and upon the details of public opinion, but it directs the manners of the community, and by regulating domestic life it regulates the State.

In the United States the influence of religion is not confined to the manners, but it extends to the intelligence of the people. Among the Anglo-Americans, there are some who profess the doctrines of Christianity from a sincere belief in them, and others who do the same because they are afraid to be suspected of unbelief. Christianity, therefore, reigns without any obstacle, by universal consent; the consequence is, as I have before observed, that every principle of the moral world is fixed and determinate, although the political world is abandoned to the debates and the experiments of men. Thus the human mind is never left to wander across a boundless field; and, whatever may be its pretensions, it is checked from time to time by barriers which it cannot surmount. Before it can perpetrate innovation, certain primal and immutable principles are laid down, and the boldest conceptions of human device are subjected to certain forms which retard and stop their completion.

The imagination of the Americans, even in its greatest flights, is circumspect and undecided; its impulses are checked, and its works unfinished. These habits of restraint recur in political society, and are singularly favorable both to the tranquillity of the people and to the durability of the institutions it has established. Nature and circumstances concurred to make the inhabitants of the United States bold men, as is sufficiently attested by the enterprising spirit with which they seek for fortune. If the mind of the Americans were free from all trammels, they would very shortly become the most daring innovators and the most implacable disputants in the world. But the revolutionists of America are obliged to profess an ostensible respect for Christian morality and equity, which does not easily permit them to violate the laws that oppose their designs; nor would they find it easy to surmount the scruples of their partisans, even if they were able to get over their own. Hitherto no one in the United States has dared to advance the maxim that everything is permissible with a view to the interests of society; an impious adage which seems to have been invented in an age of freedom to shelter all the tyrants of future ages. Thus while the law permits the Americans to do what they please, religion prevents them from conceiving, and forbids them to commit, what is rash or unjust.

Religion in America takes no direct part in the government of society, but nevertheless it must be regarded as the foremost of the political institutions of that country; for if it does not impart a taste for freedom, it facilitates the use of free institutions. Indeed, it is in this same point of view that the inhabitants of the United States themselves look upon religious belief. I do not know whether all the Americans have a sincere faith in their religion, for who can search the human heart? but I am certain that they hold it to be indispensable to the maintenance of republican institutions. This opinion is not peculiar to a class of citizen or to a party, but it belongs to the whole nation, and to every rank of society.

In the United States, if a political character attacks a sect, this may not prevent even the partisans of that very sect from supporting him; but if he attacks all the sects together, every one abandons him, and he remains alone.

While I was in America, a witness, who happened to be called at the assizes of the county of Westchester (State of New York), declared that he did not believe in the existence of God, or in the immortality of the soul. The judge refused to admit his evidence, on the ground that the witness had destroyed beforehand all the confidence of the court in what he was about to say. The newspapers related the fact without any further comment.

The Americans combine the notions of Christianity and of liberty so intimately in their minds that it is impossible to make them conceive the one without the other, and with them this conviction does not spring from that barren traditionary faith which seems to vegetate in the soul rather than to live.

The philosophers of the eighteenth century explained the gradual decay of religious faith in a very simple manner. Religious zeal, said they, must necessarily fail, the more generally liberty is established and knowledge diffused. Unfortunately, facts are by no means in accordance with their theory. There are certain populations in Europe whose unbelief is only equaled by their ignorance and their debasement, while in America one of the freest and most enlightened nations in the world fulfils all the outward duties of religion with fervor.

Upon my arrival in the United States, the religious aspect of the country was the first thing that struck my attention; and the longer I stayed there the more did I perceive the great political consequences resulting from this state of things, to which I was unaccustomed. In France I had almost always seen the spirit of religion and the spirit of freedom pursuing courses diametrically opposed to each other; but in America I found that they were intimately united, and that they reigned in common over the same country. My desire to discover the causes of this phenomenon increased from day to day. In order to satisfy it I questioned the members of all the different sects; and I more especially sought the society of the clergy, who are the depositaries of the different persuasions, and who are more especially interested in their duration. As a member of the Roman Catholic Church I was more particularly brought into contact with several of its priests, with whom I became intimately acquainted. To each of these men I expressed my astonishment and I explained my doubts; I found that they differed upon matters of detail alone; and that they mainly attributed the peaceful dominion of religion in their country to the separation of Church and State. I do not hesitate to affirm that during my stay in America I did not meet with a single individual, of the clergy or of the laity, who was not of the same opinion upon this point.

This led me to examine more attentively than I had hitherto done, the station which the American clergy occupy in political society. I learned with surprise that they filled no public appointments; not one of them is to be met with in the administration, and they are not even represented in the legislative assemblies. In several States the law excludes them from political life, public opinion in all. And when I came to inquire into the prevailing spirit of the clergy, I found that most of its members seemed to retire of their own accord from the exercise of power, and that they made it the pride of their profession to abstain from politics.

I have shown elsewhere how the American clergy stand aloof from secular affairs. This is the most obvious, but it is not the only, example of their self-restraint. In America religion is a distinct sphere, in which the priest is sovereign, but out of which he takes care never to go. Within its limits he is the master of the mind; beyond them, he leaves men to themselves, and surrenders them to the independence and instability which belong to their nature and their age. I have seen no country in which Christianity is clothed with fewer forms, figures, and observances than in the United States; or where it presents more distinct, more simple, or more general notions to the mind. Although the Christians of America are divided into a multitude of sects, they all look upon their religion in the same light. This applies to Roman Catholicism as well as to the other forms of belief. There are no Romish priests who show less taste for the minute individual observances, for extraordinary or peculiar means of salvation, or who cling more to the spirit, and less to the letter of the law, than the Roman Catholic priests of the United States. Nowhere is that doctrine of the Church, which prohibits the worship reserved to God alone from being offered to the Saints, more clearly inculcated or more generally followed. Yet the Roman Catholics of America are very submissive and very sincere.

Another remark is applicable to the clergy of every communion. The American ministers of the Gospel do not attempt to draw or to fix all the thoughts of man upon the life to come; they are willing to surrender a portion of his heart to the cares of the present; seeming to consider the goods of this world as important, although as secondary, objects. If they take no part themselves in productive labor, they are at least interested in its progression, and ready to applaud its results; and while they never cease to point to the other world as the great object of the hopes and fears of the believer, they do not forbid him honestly to court prosperity in this. Far from attempting to show that these things are distinct and contrary to one another, they study rather to find out on what point they are most nearly and closely connected.

All the American clergy know and respect the intellectual supremacy exercised by the majority; they never sustain any but necessary conflicts with it. They take no share in the altercations of parties, but they readily adopt the general opinions of their country and their age; and they allow themselves to be borne away without opposition in the current of feeling and opinion by which everything around them is carried along. They endeavor to amend their contemporaries, but they do not quite fellowship with them. Public opinion is therefore never hostile to them; it rather supports and protects them; and their belief owes its authority at the same time to the strength which is its own, and to that which they borrow from the opinions of the majority.

Thus it is that, by respecting all democratic tendencies not absolutely contrary to herself, and by making use of several of them for her own purposes, Religion sustains an advantageous struggle with that spirit of individual independence which is her most dangerous antagonist.

12

Andrew Reed

Andrew Reed (1787–1862) was an English dissenting minister and philanthropist. He was ordained in 1811 and served the same congregation, at Wycliffe Chapel, until a year before his death. Much of his time was devoted to what would now be called "fund raising" for the orphanages and other charitable institutions he established. In 1834 he was sent to America by the Congregational Union of England and Wales as a fraternal delegate to the Congregational churches of America. The real object of the visit seems to have been twofold: to discover what means of joint action existed in America among theoretically autonomous congregations, and to assess the effectiveness of voluntary church support. Reed, who received an honorary doctor of divinity degree from Yale in the process, was accompanied on the trip by Rev. James Matheson. Their findings and conclusions were published later the same year. An American edition appeared in 1835.

[*from* AMERICAN CHURCHES]

LET me now proceed to remark on that portion of Religious Economy which may be denominated *temporal*. So far as it is needful to notice it, the subject may, perhaps, be comprised under the heads of *edifices—tenure of churches—means of general support.* . . .

I am now to refer you to the *tenure* of ecclesiastical property. You are to understand that there are two bodies that are recognized by the law as holding, and claiming to hold, such property. They are the church and the parish; and they are both *corporate* bodies. The church is precisely what it is with us. The parish denoted place as well as persons; it now, by the legal changes that have been effected, denotes persons rather than place. The persons in this relation, who are deemed the parish, are the subscribers; and the term, therefore, is nearly synonymous with our term congregation, as distinguished from church. The church has the right to choose the minister; but the parish have a veto on the choice.[1] Commonly, the majority of the parish will be in membership with the church, so that there is little danger of conflict of opinion, except in gross mischoice. The fittings and property with the edifice are considered to belong to the church; but the edifice itself is held by the parish as a corporation. The law knows not a church in its religious, but in its civil capacity; and the evidence of the existence of a civil corporation must, of course, be found in enrolment and subscriptions. Pewholders are deemed to have a separate right of property; and they can bring their action against the parish, if that property is injured. This provision is necessary, from the common practice of selling the pews as the means of meeting the first expenses of erection. What would be regarded as a fair sum is given for the purchase; and, afterwards, they bear a yearly rate, that is adequate to sustain the minister, and lesser charges.

The law has been very different, as you will suppose, at different periods; and now it varies in the several States.

I have endeavoured to express the spirit of the law; its form, under the modelling hand of time and circumstance, will not be less liberal, and will become more simple. It is certainly a great improvement in legislation on this subject. The high advantage consists in making the church, or congregation of subscribers, a body corporate. This gives them a legal being; allows them to sue, and be sued; and to uphold all their civil rights with facility. It is at once a great security in the tenure of fixed property, and a discharge from an immense standing expense, on the renewal of trusts or trust-deeds. While other interests are justly looked to, this ought not to be neglected in our own country. The present state of the law, as it affects all the Dissenting bodies, is such as not only to expose the property to serious hazard, but as to incur a charge on them of from 4000 £ to 5000 £ per annum, without benefit to any one.

The final head of temporal economy relates to the *means of support*. It has great importance in itself, and it is enhanced by the position of the church at the present time. At home, we are hardly allowed to refer to this subject, even in other connexions, without being overwhelmed with charges, which confound a good man, and make a calm and philosophical conclusion extremely difficult. However, I shall endeavour to treat the subject without acrimony and without fear; and in the hope that it may contribute to the formation of a just opinion, and, consequently, to the advancement of true religion, without respect to sect or party.

You are aware that our fathers, when they braved the Atlantic, and sought a settlement in the New World, did so for conscience' sake. But, although they fled from the face of persecution, and certainly would have recoiled from the act of direct persecution, nevertheless, they understood so little the nature of religious liberty that they established a system which would, under a change of circumstances, inevitably assume a persecuting character. In fact, this ignorance of the imprescriptible claims of conscience was not their fault in particular; it was the common fault of all, and of the time. Immunity on the one hand, and restriction or persecution on the other, were the only forms in which religion appeared: and although the principles of liberty were to be developed by the searching hand of intolerance, it was not to be expected that they should be appreciated, adopted, and matured without a considerable lapse of time and experiment. The efforts made, in these youthful settlements, in favour of prescription and endowment, and the counter efforts peacefully made in favour of perfect religious freedom, supply evidence, which is so interesting that it cannot be neglected; and so strong that prejudice itself cannot put it down.

While, in every case, the results have been the same, the methods of reaching them have been various. This makes it somewhat difficult to treat them, but it necessarily increases the power of the testimony.

In Virginia, the Episcopal church was established by law. The law was tried in both its forms; without the toleration, and afterwards with the toleration, of other sects. For nearly a century, it was the exclusive religion of the State; it was endowed, and all parties were compelled to contribute to its support. The consequence was any thing but what a good Episcopalian would desire. Unworthy and incompetent men, in search of respectability or emolument, made the church a prey. Having nothing to apprehend from the people, or the rivalry of sects, they became careless, and indolent, and frequently dissolute. The statements on this subject abound, and are most painful. The pastors generally neglected the people, and the people despised and forsook the pastors; so that the system was dead, even while it retained the visible forms of existence.

It was then tried with toleration. This alteration admitted the other sects to enter the State; and without direct hinderance, to labour for the instruction and salvation of the people. The privileged clergy, however, despised their rivals; and as all sects were still taxed for their benefit, it concerned them little by what name they were called; and they continued to repose on their supplies, in indolence and security. If they slept, the oppressed sectaries did not sleep. Their efforts were not in vain: and these, with the reckless negligence of the endowed party, and the changes effected by the Revolution, prepared the State for an improved method.

It was felt that all could no longer be made to support one; and it was proposed that all should be assessed for the benefit of all the denominations. This, however, was declined; the Dissenting bodies protesting most nobly against any participation in the benefit of such a tax. Finding them firm in the rejection of all State allowance, an act was passed in 1775, to relieve them from all contributions towards the support of the established religion;

and, eventually, the whole question was disposed of, and the whole country satisfied, by placing all denominations on one footing; by knowing them only as civil corporations, and with-holding all allowance.

As quickly after this as the circumstances would allow, the Episcopal church revived, and placed itself on equal terms with its compeers. To this time it has continued to advance. It has now fifty-five clergymen devoted to their work, who are superintend-ing affectionate and thriving flocks: and it is spreading itself on every hand, having good report amongst the people.

That we may change the field of observation, let us pass into New England. Here, the church, or Standing Order, was founded on the principle of State interference. In Massachusetts, in 1631, the General Court passed a law that all should contribute in their parishes to upholding the Standing Order; and that none should be eligible for civil office who were not in church membership. This was not only to make the people pay; but, having paid, it was to punish them by a Test Act if they did not conform. This principle was afterwards modified, by allowing persons to divert their payment to some other body, on certifying that they be-longed to it, still compelling them to pay to some religious society; and by the provisions of the Half-way Covenant. I think, so far as Massachusetts is concerned, I have shown how it affected the Congregational Order, by the corruption of doctrine; it may be proper to remark, that it extensively promoted the interests of sectarianism. Under the milder form of the compulsory payment, the worldly were obliged to pay equally with the religious; and as the worldly will always have the strongest objection to pure and undefiled religion, the chances are decidedly for error, and against truth. The worldly misbeliever, if compelled to pay either to Universalism or Calvinism, would prefer Universalism as a species of quietism; but if left to his choice to pay or not, he would say, "I will pay to neither, for I love my money better than both." Has the true church of Christ a right to compel such a man; and if it has, will any benefit accrue?

In Vermont and New Hampshire there were not only State

enactments, but provisions of land in favour of the same and similar objects. Each township had an original grant of three hundred acres. This estate was to benefit equally four parties; the church—the school—the Society for Promoting Christian Knowledge—and the *first* minister. The first minister was deemed a proprietor; and he could will his portion away to his family or friends. It was, in fact, a bonus to induce a person to encounter the first difficulty of settling; and it usually attracted the least worthy to the spot. The one fourth originally meant for the permanent uses of the church, with its other privileges, remained, and the church languished in the midst of its indulgences. It is remarkable that "the desolations" of these districts, which a Scotch writer has magnified, to illustrate the inefficiency of the voluntary principle, are the very desolations which were created by the compulsory and State methods on which I am animadverting.

The changes which have taken place have been various and gradual, but they were all in favour of the voluntary principle; and in the year 1833, only two years since, the last fragments of the compulsory and endowed system were demolished by the power of improved opinion and religious principle. This was done in Connecticut about fifteen years since, and in Vermont and New Hampshire about the same time. It was in Massachusetts it lingered till 1833; and, by a striking coincidence with what is now happening in our own country, it was upheld to the last by Unitarianism. . . .[2]

The voluntary principle, then, is the only one now for the support of these churches. It has been tried in some states to the exclusion of every other; it has been tried in other states, for different periods of time, where every other has failed; and what is the result? Deliberately, but without hesitation, I say, *the result is in everything and every where most favourable to the voluntary, and against the compulsory principle.* Let us look at this, both as a matter of testimony, and as a matter of fact.

Testimony is universally in its favour. Let me not be mistaken. Some may carp at the term universal, and endeavour to muster some few voices in favour of the Standing order. Such voices are doubtless to be heard; but it is truly marvellous that they are so few. Of course, the transition so lately effected from one system to the other must have disturbed many interests, and have brought loss to some. It was to be expected that some, under the old system, would be incompetent; and these would naturally incline to an allowance from the state rather than from the people, who would be too wise to grant it. Some who had become gray and infirm under that system, might be supposed to cling to it, even though every advantage were with the change. Harvey showed his skill in metaphysics, as well as in physics, when he observed that none of his profession above forty years of age received his theory, or were to be expected to receive it.

But, in truth, though every reasonable mind would be ready to make considerable allowances for the influence of such causes, it was never less necessary; and they are only referred to, to prevent captious and unfair objection. After having invited the most candid opinion on the subject; after having sincerely sought for the truth, whether favourable or unfavourable to the voluntary system; and, after having sought this in every quarter, and chiefly where state provisions had been enjoyed; I certainly did not find half a dozen men who would give their suffrages for the old method! The ministers, as a body, who might be supposed to have professionally strong preferences to a fixed and compulsory stipend, were united in their attachment to the voluntary principle. The brethren in Massachusetts, where the change had been so recently completed, rejoiced in it, and anticipated from it a decided advance in pure religion. Those of New Hampshire, Vermont, and Maine, with whom we had an opportunity of meeting and conferring, were unanimous in the same judgement, and referred gratefully the renovated state of their churches and of the ministry to its benign influence. The brethren of Connecticut, whom we met in large numbers, decidedly concurred in the same opinion. The Episcopalian of Virginia, and the Congregationalist of New England, who had been indulged and protected to the utmost, were equally in favour of the new principle. Men of every denomination, the Methodist, the Baptist, the Presbyterian, the Reformed, the Lutheran, the Churchman, and the Independent, all deprecate state interference and state allowance. Men of every region, the East, the West, the North, the South, and who are most deeply concerned for the interests of religion, agree in coming to the same conclusion. Indeed, such unanimity of opinion on a practical question, involving the interests of so many parties, and to be determined mostly by those whose habits and thoughts had been associated only with the old system, is what I never expected to find. It assured me of at least two things. 1. That the evil of this system must have been great, indeed, and visible to all. And, 2. That these devoted men had wisdom enough and piety enough at once to resolve that what was injurious to religion could not be beneficial to them. . . .

Then, Fact is unanimously in its favour. This submits a wide field to us, and the difficulty is, still to condense observation. Let me dispose, first, of New England. It has undergone a most felicitous improvement since the alterations. I need not, I presume, enter into detail on this particular; for none will arise to contradict the assertion. The Standing Order could not have stood its ground as a State establishment. It was inert and inefficient; the Dissenting Community on the one hand, and infidelity on the other, were prevailing against it; while, within itself, was engendered the worst forms of heresy. It is now placed on a level with its rivals, and it is equal to the best in the race of excellence. Every form of orthodoxy has made a surprising start, and is sustaining it as it was begun. The ministry has been supplied with better men; the men have been better maintained. Churches have been revived where they languished, and they have been created in abundance where they did not exist. The "desolations" of New England, which have been triumphantly cited from reports many years old, are rapidly disappearing under the voluntary principle, and never were the prospects on the future, for that favoured land, so bright and hopeful as they are at the present time.

I think I have already shown, with some clearness, *how much of her prosperity* New England owes to the principle of a Standing Order; I must now bring the means possessed by other States into comparison with those she is admitted to enjoy. Massachusetts, then, the principal State of New England, and the longest settled, has—

Population	610,014	Churches	600
Ministers	704	Communicants	73,264

New York, which is the principal middle State, and which has advanced with more rapidity than any of the other States, and which, therefore, has had the greater difficulty in meeting the spiritual wants of the people, has—

Population	1,913,508	Churches	1,800
Ministers	1,750	Communicants ...	184,583

Is this a sign of desolation?
Pennsylvania, the next middle State of consideration, has—

Population	1,347,672	Churches	1,829
Ministers	1,133	Communicants ...	180,205

Is this a sign of desolation? If it is, what are we to say of the most favoured divisions of our own country? Scotland is universally thought to be highly privileged in her religious means; but Scotland stands thus—

Population	2,365,807	Churches	1,804
Ministers	1,765	Communicants (uncertain)	

But it will be objected that these States are not either of the West or South, and are, therefore, not to be accepted in evidence on the wants of the more distant regions. I admit this; but, with this admission, I maintain that it is unjust to make the condition of the young States in the West, or the Slave States in the South, which are just colonizing, the test of the voluntary principle, as compared with New England; as unjust as it would be to try the compulsory principle in Great Britain, not by what it had wrought there, but by what it had done in Jamaica and in the

27661

Canadas. Having, in mere justice, protested against this mode of trial, I am not, on that account, unwilling to make the comparison.
Tennessee has—

Population	684,000	*Churches*	630
Ministers	458	*Communicants*	60,000

Ohio, a Western State, which, in 1810, had only a population of 230,000, and forty years since, not more than five hundred persons settled, has now a population of 937,000, scattered over a surface of 40,000 square miles, nearly the size of England and Wales. With these disadvantages, the account stands thus—

Population	937,000	*Churches*	802
Ministers	841	*Communicants*	76,460

Indiana, which is further West, and is settling at this very time, has, while struggling with the first difficulties of the forest, found leisure and means to provide itself as follows—

Population	341,000	*Churches*	440
Ministers	340	*Communicants*	34,826

Is this, then, the desolation of the West? If so, what a moral desolation must Scotland be? In truth, are not these figures, in union with such circumstances, most astonishing? I confess to you that I have looked at them once and again; and when I have assured myself that there is no cause to doubt their correctness, it still appears next to impossible for a people, settling in this new land, without aid from Government, and spread over so large a surface, to have achieved so great a work for their spiritual welfare.

I have travelled over a large portion of the West, and I can readily account for the impressions which have been received by strangers in those regions. The eye is disappointed at not seeing, amidst every little cluster of log cabins, the spire or tower of the village church; the people who do not profess religion are not careful to save appearances, and you quickly see them as they are;

the ministry, as a distinct order, is far less apparent than in the East, for those who minister among the Methodists and Baptists are mostly without regular training. But it is evident that he who is not prepared to revise and correct his impressions, under such circumstances, is not qualified to report concerning them. The ministers here are in advance of the people; they will still keep in advance of them; and it would be the desire of ambition, not of wisdom, that would place them so far in advance as to be out of reach, and out of sight. The little churches also in the scattered districts bear the same relation to the state of the people. They are frequently log cabins, and have no outward sign to designate their use; but as the log cabin yields to better accommodations in domestic life, so surely does the church receive an improved and visible form. In fact, the West is not New England. There are fewer means; they are of a lower character; and the people who do not profess are less under the influence of wholesome restraint and decorum. How can it be otherwise? There is, undoubtedly, much to be done for it. But, meantime, you will know how to judge of the reports made on its waste places by remembering that, if its present means are fewer than those of New England, they are decidedly more than those of Scotland.

If we turn from the particular and comparative views, with which I have thus supplied you, to those which are more general, the American Institutions suffer nothing. The severest trial that can by possibility be made on this subject is to take the ten States, on which we have any safe returns, which have been *last added* to the Commonwealth. These are Kentucky, Tennessee, Ohio, Indiana, Illinois, Alabama, Mississippi, Missouri, Louisiana, and Florida. These will give a return of persons spread over a surface of 480,670 square miles, about nine times the size of England and Wales, as follows—

Population	3,641,000	*Churches*	3,701
Ministers	2,690	*Communicants* ...	286,560

Need I say how greatly this again exceeds Scotland!

If we take the principal towns of that country, and put them into comparison with those of ours, the advantage is entirely with them. For instance, Liverpool has—

Population 210,000	*Churches* 67
Ministers 57	*Communicants* 18,000

but New York, which is its counterpart, has—

Population 230,000	*Churches* 132
Ministers 142	*Communicants* 31,337

Edinburgh has—

Population 150,000	*Churches* 65
Ministers 70	*Communicants (uncertain)*

but Philadelphia has—

Population 200,000	*Churches* 83
Ministers 137	*Communicants (uncertain)*

Glasgow has—

Population 220,000	*Churches* 74
Ministers 76	*Communicants (uncertain)*

but Boston has—

Population 60,000	*Churches* 55
Ministers 57	*Communicants (uncertain)*

Nottingham has—

Population 50,000	*Churches* 23
Ministers 23	*Communicants* 4,864

but Cincinnati, a city only forty years old, and in the forests, has—

Population 30,000	*Churches* 21
Ministers 22	*Communicants* 8,555

After the statements already made, there can be no difficulty in concluding that the general supply of the whole country is, in comparison with any other country, astonishingly great. The figures would stand thus—

| *Population* .... *13,000,000* | *Churches* ...... *12,580* |
| *Ministers* ..... *11,450* | *Communicants* .. *1,550,890* |

This yields about one clergyman and one church to every thousand persons; while it gives about one in nine of the whole population as in a state of communion; and as the returns do not include the communicants connected with the Episcopal, the Catholic, and some smaller sects, it is certainly not taken too high. Of England, if it is allowed that there are seven thousand working clergy in the Episcopal church, and five or six thousand clergy united to other divisions of the church, the amount of ministers will bear about the same proportion to the population as in America. But if this ministry is to be submitted to the two indispensable tests of its efficiency on the people, church accommodation and church communicants, it will fail most lamentably. The Bishop of London, in his evidence on this subject, states that certainly *not one tenth* of the people are supplied with churchroom in the places of his diocese. I conclude that no diocese can exceed that of London, and take the whole therefore at one tenth. If it is conceded that the Dissenters supply as much as the Episcopal church, I suppose this is the utmost that may be asked. This, then, would supply both by the voluntary and compulsory system only an accommodation for *one fifth of the people.*

Then look at the state of communion, which is, after all, the real test of strength and influence. It is shown by documents, which will not be disputed, that the Episcopal church, though hers is a *free* communion, has only 350,000 communicants. I think the communicants of the Dissenting bodies may be safely put down at 700,000; and I do not expect more will be allowed to them. This, however, will only give us 1,050,000; while America, at a low estimate, and with a universally *strict* communion, has 1,550,890; an increase on ours of more than one third!

All these results are most striking; and, in truth, if they are admitted, they are overwhelming in evidence. On this account, the Statistical Returns have recently been put into dispute, and have been taxed with the grossest exaggerations. That some exaggerated statements have been hastily made, I am ready to allow, for I have seen such. But I have given much attention to the approved documentary evidence, and have sought, in several cases, to verify or shake it; and the result is that I am fully persuaded it deserves confidence. Great pains have, indeed, been taken with this class of evidence. All the denominations have more association and more system than are common with us. They make their yearly returns in their respective associations where they are known, and where serious error would be corrected. These are made again to conventions, or central bodies. General almanacks are prepared for public use, into which these statistics are introduced, and are subject to revision and amendment. One gentleman, with excellent capacities for the subject, and of unquestioned integrity, has devoted himself entirely to these important inquiries. All the annual and local returns have been searched and sifted by him; and they have appeared, in the amended form, in the *Quarterly Register*, a work which, for its research and fidelity, has acquired high repute in all the denominations; and it is the interest of each body to see that no other body is allowed, at its expense, to pass with exaggerated numbers. I say not that these returns, after all the pains taken, are perfect; but I fearlessly say that they are both honest and admirable. Certainly we have to this day no returns, dissenting or episcopal, ecclesiastical or civil, that can in any way be compared with them. With us, it is still a desideratum, which, I trust, some one will at length supply.

On the whole, then, the conclusion is that whatever trivial errors may cleave to a subject which does not admit of perfect exactness, the general results remain indisputable. And with such results before us, shall we still, with blindness and prejudice, refuse the lessons they imperatively convey? While such evidence is developing itself in favour of the voluntary principle, where alone it has found an open and fair field of probation, should not the Dissenter be confirmed in his assurance of its power and efficiency; and be disposed to rest his cause on it with confidence and quiet?

And should not the pious Churchman, who regards an establishment only as it promotes the interests of religion amongst the people, be inclined, whatever may have been his original disinclination, to weigh such testimony with calm and dispassionate attention? At least, he should know that he need not be withheld from the subject by apprehension and alarm. The Dissenter concerns not himself in the temporal estate of the church, except as it may affect his equality as a citizen, and as he devoutly desires that the Episcopal portion of the church may arrive at a condition most favourable to her honour, stability, and usefulness. Spoliation not only is not, it never can be his object; for he can never profit by the spoil. Even the paltry grant, passing under the name of the Regium Donum, his principles, fairly carried out, compel him to decline. Whatever emoluments may be granted by the State to others, and whatever his opinion of them, he deems himself richer than they in having none; for the church and the world are to be renovated, not by patronage, but by principles. At all events, if the infirmities of our common nature should allow no more in the present period of excitement, this improved conviction might take from our discussions most of their bitterness while they continue, and conduct us the more quickly to peace when they terminate. How apposite and beautiful, at such a time, is the prayer of the excellent Venn, of Huddersfield: "O, Prince of Peace, heal our divisions! Diffuse thy patient loving Spirit! Give discernment to distinguish aright between what is essential and what is not, and (meekness) to bear with each other's differences, till the perfect day discovers all things in their true proportions." . . .

It must be evident to a practised judgment that this aptitude to become all things to all men and all occasions is a valuable qualification for real usefulness, in a country where the form and fashion of things are continually varying under the influence of increasing civilization and refinement. The free institutions of the people possess just the same pliancy. The *principle of adaptation*, the want of which a high authority has lately admitted to be the great defect of an Establishment, is certainly the life and virtue of the voluntary system. Whatever may otherwise be its character, its adversaries cannot disallow the inherent power of adaptation; and if they did, America would confound them. The school-house and the church are seen to accommodate themselves precisely to the state of the people, never behind them, never too much in advance. Their very form and structure pass through the gradations of wood, brick, and stone, as do the residences of the people; and their lessons are dispensed by "line upon line and precept upon precept, here a little, and there much," as they can bear them. . . .

Who shall doubt of such a people? They are full of hope themselves, and they create hope in others. Every thing about them contributes to nourish it. They are born into national existence in the most auspicious times. All the lessons of wisdom which have been suggested through ages to other nations are at their command. They begin their course just where other empires have closed theirs. Their field of action is so vast that they may put forth the mightiest energies, without exposure to hostile interests and barbarous warfare. They need fear no foe, and therefore they need not embarrass themselves with alliances which might lead to conflict and bloodshed. They have the fairest opportunity of showing how little a Government may be felt as a burden, and how much as a blessing, silently diffusing life, liberty, and joy, over an immense community. The people are aware of this, and are ennobled by their circumstances. They believe all things, and they will accomplish all things.

Yes, they will accomplish all things, with the single provision, that *they remain under the influence of religion*. Religion is requisite to the welfare of any people; but they have made it emphatically necessary, not only to their prosperity, but to their political existence. The evils to which their promising circumstances chiefly expose them are worldliness and presumption; and these can be quelled only by religion. No approaches to the experiment they are now making on the liberty of the subject have been made with success; and they can only succeed by making religion their best ally. Universal suffrage, whatever may be its abstract merits or demerits, is neither desirable nor possible, except the people are the subjects of universal education and universal piety. AMERICA WILL BE GREAT IF AMERICA IS GOOD. If not, her greatness will vanish away like a morning cloud.

NOTES

[1] In 1820, the Supreme Court of Massachusetts ruled in the Dedham case (*Baker v. Fales*) that the control of property and the authority to hire a minister rested with the citizens of the town (i.e., "parish" in Reed's usage) rather than with the communicants ("church"). See Stokes, III, pp. 377–382 and Mark De Wolfe Howe, *Cases on Church and State in the United States* (Cambridge: Harvard University Press, 1952), pp. 40–54.

[2] The evolution of constitutional guarantees of religious freedom in the several states is discussed in Anson Phelps Stokes, *Church and State in the United States* (New York: Harper, 1950), three volumes, Vol. I, pp. 358–446.

13

Harriet Martineau

Harriet Martineau (1802–1876) was already well known in
England at the time of her visit to the United States. Her
education had been irregular and haphazard, but the *Illustra-
tions of Political Economy* (1834), a popularization of the
liberal economic doctrines of Mill, Ricardo, and Malthus established her securely in English literary circles. The American
visit (1834–1836) was intended largely as a respite, but she
characteristically became deeply and personally involved in the
abolitionist movement, which was then in an early and quite
unpopular stage. *Society in America* was written shortly upon
her return, and richly deserves its reputation as one of the two
or three best books on America written in the nineteenth
century. The book contains such a shrewd appraisal of the
strengths and weaknesses of the voluntary church that I have
excerpted from it at somewhat greater length than from others.

[*from* SOCIETY IN AMERICA]

R ELIGION is the highest fact in the Rights of Man from its
being the most exclusively private and individual, while it is also
a universal, concern, of any in which man is interested. Religion
is, in its widest sense, "the tendency of human nature to the
Infinite"; and its principle is manifested in the pursuit of perfection in any direction whatever. It is in this widest sense that some
speculative atheists have been religious men; religious in their
efforts after self-perfection; though unable to personify their

109

conception of the Infinite. In a somewhat narrower sense, religion is the relation which the highest human sentiments bear towards an infinitely perfect Being.

There can be no further narrowing than this. Any account of religion which restricts it within the boundaries of any system, which connects it with any mode of belief, which implicates it with hope of reward or fear of punishment, is low and injurious, and debases religion into superstition.

The Christian religion is specified as being the highest fact in the rights of man from its embodying (with all the rest) the principle of natural religion—that religion is at once an individual, an universal, and an equal concern. In it may be found a sanction of all just claims of political and social equality; for it proclaims, now in music and now in thunder—it blazons, now in sunshine and now in lightning—the fact of the natural equality of men. In giving forth this as its grand doctrine, it is indeed "the root of all democracy," the root of the maxim (among others) that among the inalienable rights of all men are life, liberty, and the pursuit of happiness. The democracy of America is planted down deep into the christian religion; into its principles, which it has in common with natural religion, and which it vivifies and illumines, but does not alter.

How does the existing state of religion accord with the promise of its birth? In a country which professes to secure to every man the pursuit of happiness in his own way, what is the state of his liberty in the most private and individual of all concerns? How carefully are all men and women left free from interference in following up their own aspirations after the Infinite, in realising their own ideas of perfection, in bringing into harmonious action the functions of their spirits, as infinitely diversified as the expression of their features?

The absence of such diversity is the first striking fact which presents itself on the institution of such an inquiry. If there were no constraint—no social reward or penalty—such an approach to uniformity of profession could not exist as is seen in the United States. In a society where speculation and profession were left perfectly free, as included among the inalienable rights of man, there would be many speculative (though probably extremely few practical) atheists; there would be an adoption by many of the principles of natural religion, otherwise than in and through Christianity; and Christianity would be adopted in modes as various as the minds by which it would be recognised. Instead of this, we find laws framed against speculative atheists: opprobrium directed upon such as embrace natural religion otherwise than through Christianity: and a yet more bitter oppression exercised by those who view Christianity in one way, over those who regard it in another. A religious young christian legislator was pitied, blamed, and traduced in Boston, last year, by clergymen, lawyers, and professors of a college, for endeavouring to obtain a repeal of the law under which the testimony of speculative atheists is rejected in courts of justice; Quakers (calling themselves Friends) excommunicate each other; Presbyterian clergymen preach hatred to Catholics; a convent is burnt, and the nuns are banished from the neighborhood;[1] and Episcopalian clergymen claim credit for admitting Unitarians to sit in committees for public objects! As might be expected under such an infringement of the principle of securing to every man the pursuit of happiness in his own way, there is no such endless diversity in the action of minds, and utterance of tongues, as nature and fidelity to truth peremptorily demand. Truth is deprived of the irrefragable testimony which would be afforded by whatever agreement might arise amidst this diversity; religion is insulted and scandalised by nominal adherence and hypocritical advocacy. There are many ways of professing Christianity in the United States: but there are few, very few men, whether speculative or thoughtless, whether studious or ignorant, whether reverent or indifferent, whether sober or profligate, whether disinterested or worldly, who do not carefully profess Christianity, in some form or another. This, as men are made, is unnatural. Society presents no faithful mirror of the religious perspective of the human mind.

It may be asked whether this is not true of the Old World also.

It is. But the society of the Old World has not yet grasped in practice any one fundamental democratic principle; and the few who govern the many have not yet perceived that religion is "the root of all democracy"; they are so far from it that they are still upholding an established form of religion; in which a particular mode of belief is enforced upon minds by the imposition of virtual rewards and punishments. The Americans have long taken higher ground; repudiating establishments, and professing to leave religion free. They must be judged by their own principles, and not by the example of societies whose errors they have practically denounced by their adoption of the Voluntary Principle.

The almost universal profession in America of the adoption of Christianity—this profession by many whose habits of thought, and others whose habits of living forbid the supposition that it is the religion of their individual intellects and affections—compels the inquiry what sort of Christianity it is that is professed, and how it is come by. There is no evading the conviction that it is to a vast extent a monstrous superstition that is thus embraced by the tyrant, the profligate, the worldling, the bigot, the coward, and the slave; a superstition which offers little molestation to their vices, little rectification to their errors; a superstition which is but the spurious offspring of that divine Christianity which "is the root of all democracy, the highest fact in the Rights of Man." That so many of the meek, pure, disinterested, free, and brave, make the same profession proves only that they penetrate to religion through superstition; or that they cast away unconsciously the superstition with which their spirits have no affinity, and accept such truth as all superstition must include in order to live. . . .

If religion springs from morals, the religion must be most faulty where the morals are so. The greatest fault in American morals is an excessive regard to opinion. This is the reason of the want of liberality of which unbelievers, and unusual believers, have so much reason to complain. But the spirit of religion is already bursting through sectarian restraints. Many powerful voices are raised, within the churches as well as out of them, and even from a few pulpits, against the mechanical adoption and practice of religion, and in favour of individuality of thought, and the consequent spontaneousness of speech and action. Many indubitable Christians are denouncing cant as strongly as those whom cant has alienated from Christianity. The dislike of associations for religious objects is spreading fast; and the eyes of multitudes are being opened to the fact that there can be little faith at the bottom of that craving for sympathy which prevents men and women from cheerfully doing their duty to God and their neighbour unless sanctioned by a crowd. Some of the clergy have done away with the forms of admission to their churches which were formerly considered indispensable. There is a visible reaction in the best part of society in favour of any man who stands alone on any point of religious concern: and though such an one has the more regularly drilled churches against him, he is usually cheered by the grasp of some trusty right hand of fellowship.

The eagerness in pursuit of speculative truth is shown by the rapid sale of every kind of heretical work. The clergy complain of the enormous spread of bold books, from the infidel tract to the latest handling of the miracle question, as sorrowfully as the most liberal members of society lament the unlimited circulation of the false morals issued by certain Religious Tract Societies. Both testify to the interest taken by the people in religion. The love of truth is also shown by the outbreak of heresy in all directions. There are schisms among all the more strict of the religious bodies, and large secessions and new formations among those which are bound together by slight forms. There are even a few places to be found where Deists may come among Christians to worship their common Father, without fear of insult to their feelings, and mockery of their convictions.

I know also of one place, at least, and I believe there are now several, where the people of colour are welcome to worship with the whites, actually intermingled with them, instead of being set apart in a gallery appropriated to them. This is the last possible test of the conviction of human equality entertained by the white worshippers. It is such a test of this, their christian conviction, as no persons of any rank in England are ever called upon to abide. I think it very probable that the course of action which is common in America will be followed in this instance. A battle for a principle is usually fought long, and under discouragement: but the sure fruition is almost instantaneous, when the principle is but once put into action. The people of colour do actually, in one or more religious assemblies, sit among the whites, in token that the principle of human brotherhood is fully admitted. It may be anticipated that the example will spread from church to church—in the rural districts of the north first, and then in the towns,* so that the clergy will soon find themselves released from the necessity of veiling, or qualifying, the most essential truth of the gospel, from the pastoral consideration for the passions and prejudices of the white portion of their flocks, which they at present plead in excuse of their compromise.

The noble beneficence of the whole community shows that the spirit of the gospel is in the midst of them, as it respects the condition of the poor, ignorant, and afflicted. Of the generosity of society there can be no question; and if it were only accompanied with the strict justice which the same principles of christian charity require; if there were as zealous a regard to the rights of intellect and conscience in all as to the wants and sufferings of the helpless, such a realisation of high morals would be seen as the world has not yet beheld. I have witnessed sights which persuade me that the principle of charity will yet be carried out to its full extent. It gave me pleasure to see the provisions made for every class of unfortunates. It gave me more

* When I visited the New York House of Refuge for the reformation of juvenile delinquents, one of the officers showed me, with complacency, that children of colour were sitting among the whites, in both the boys' and girls' schools. On explaining to me afterwards the arrangements of the chapel he pointed out the division appropriated to the pupils of colour. "Do you let them mix in school, and separate them at worship?" I asked. He replied, with no little sharpness, "We are not amalgamationists, madam." The absurdity of the sudden wrath, and of the fact of a distinction being made at worship (of all occasions) which was not made elsewhere, was so palpable, that the whole of our large party burst into irresistible laughter.

to see young men and women devoting their evening and Sunday leisure to fostering, in the most benignant manner, the minds of active and trustful children. But nothing gave me so much delight as what was said by a young physician to a young clergyman, on their entering a new building prepared as a place of worship for children, and also as a kind of school: as a place where religion might have its free course among young and free minds. "Now," said the young physician, "here we are, with these children dependent upon us. Never let us defile this place with the smallest act of spiritual tyranny. Watch me, and I will watch you, that we may not lay the weight of a hair upon these little minds. If we impose one single opinion upon them, we bring a curse upon our work. Here, in this one place, let minds be absolutely free." This is the true spirit of reverence. He who spoke those words may be considered, I believe and trust, as the organ of no few, who are aware that reverence is as requisite to the faithful administration of charity, as to the acceptable offering of prayer. . . .

The inquiry concerning the working of the voluntary system in America—the only country where it operates without an establishment by its side—takes two directions. It is asked, first, whether religion is administered sufficiently to the people; and, secondly, what is the character of the clergy.

The first question is easily answered. The eagerness for religious instruction and the means of social worship are so great that funds and buildings are provided wherever society exists. Though the clergy bear a larger proportion to men of other occupations, I believe, than is the case anywhere, except perhaps in the Peninsula, they are too few for the religious wants of the people. Men are wanting; but churches and funds are sufficient. According to a general summary of religious denominations, made in 1835, the number of churches or congregations was 15,477; the population being, exclusive of the slaves, between fifteen and sixteen millions; and a not inconsiderable number being settlers scattered in places too remote for the formation of regular societies, with settled ministers. To these 15,477 churches there were only 12,130 ministers. If to these settled clergy there are added the licentiates and candidates of the Presbyterian church, the local preachers of the Methodists, the theological students, and quaker administrators, it will be acknowledged that the number of religious teachers bears an unusually large proportion to the population. Yet the Baptist sect alone proclaims a want of above three thousand ministers to supply the existing churches. Every exertion is made to meet the religious wants of the people. The American Education Society has assisted largely in sending forth young ministers; the Mission and Bible Societies exhibit large results. In short, society in the United States offers every conceivable testimony that the religious instincts of the people may be trusted to supply their religious wants. It is only within four or five years that this has been fully admitted even in the State of Massachusetts. Up to 1834, every citizen of that State was obliged to contribute something to the support of some sect or church. The inconsistency of this obligation with true democratic principle was then fully perceived, and religion left wholly to voluntary support. It is needless to say that the event has fully justified the confidence of those who have faith enough in Christianity to see that it needs no protection from the State, but will commend itself to human hearts better without.

As to the other particular of the inquiry—the character of the clergy—more is to be said.

It is clear that there is no room under the voluntary system for some of the worst characteristics which have disgraced all christian priesthoods. In America, there can be no grasping after political power; no gambling in a lottery of church livings; no worldly pomp and state. These sins are precluded under a voluntary system, in the midst of a republic. Instead of these things, we find the protestant clergy generally belonging to the federal party, when they open their lips upon politics at all. They belong to the apprehensive party; according to all precedent. It would be called strange if it did not almost universally happen, that (with the exception of the political churchmen of the Old World) they who uphold a faith which shall remove mountains, who teach that men are not to fear "them that kill the body, and afterwards have no more that they can do," are the most timid class of society; the most backward in all great conflicts of principles. They have ever rested invisible in their tents, when any wrestling was going on between morals and abuses. They have ever, as a body, belonged to the aristocratic and fearing party. So it is in America, where the fearing party is depressed; as it has ever been where the aristocratic party is uppermost.

The clergy in America are not, as a body, seekers of wealth. It is so generally out of their reach that the adoption of the clerical profession is usually an unequivocal testimony to their disinterestedness about money. I say "usually," because there are exceptions. The profession has been one of such high honour that it rises to an equality with wealth. It is common, not to say usual, that young clergymen, who are almost invariably from poor families, marry ladies of fortune. Where there are several sisters in a rich family, it seems to be regarded as a matter of course that one will marry a clergyman. Amidst some good which arises out of this practice, there is the enormous evil, not peculiar to America, that adventurers are tempted into the profession. Not a few planters in the south began life as poor clergymen, and obtained by marriage the means of becoming planters. Not a few pastors in the north grow more sleek than they ever were saintly, and go through two safe and quiet preachments on Sundays, as the price of their week-day ease. But, as long as the salaries of ministers are so moderate as they now are, it cannot be otherwise than that the greater number of clergy enter upon their profession in full view of a life of labour, with small pecuniary recompense. There can, I think, be no question that the vocation is adopted from motives as pure as often actuate men; and that the dangers to which the clergy succumb arise afterwards out of their disadvantageous position.

It is to be wished that some alteration could be made in the mode of remunerating the clergy. At present, they have usually small salaries and large presents. Nothing is more natural than that grateful individuals or flocks should like to testify their respect for their pastor by adding to his comforts and luxuries:

but, if all the consequences were considered, I think the practice would be forborne, and the salary increased instead. In the present state of morals, it happens that instances are rare where one person can give pecuniary benefit to another without injury to one or both. Sympathy, help, may be given, with great mutual profit; but rarely money or money's worth. This arises from the false associations which have been gathered round wealth, and have implicated it too extensively with mental and moral independence. Any one may answer for himself the question whether it is often possible to regard a person to whom he is under pecuniary obligation with precisely the same freedom, from first to last, which would otherwise exist. If among people of similar views, objects, and interests, this is felt as a difficulty, it is aggravated into a great moral danger when spiritual influences are to be dispensed by the aided and obliged party. I see no safety in anything short of a strict rule on the part of an honourable pastor to accept of no gift whatever. This would require some self-denial on the part of his friends; but they ought to be aware that giving gifts is the coarsest and lowest method of testifying respect and affection. Many ways are open to them: first by taking care that their pastor has such a fixed annual provision made for him as will secure him from the too heavy pressure of family cares; and then by yielding him that honest friendship, and plain-spoken sympathy (without any religious peculiarity) which may animate him in his studies and in his ministrations.

The American clergy being absolved from the common clerical vices of ambition and cupidity, it remains to be seen whether they are free also from that of the idolatry of opinion. They enter upon their office generally with pious and benevolent views. Do they retain their moral independence in it? I cannot answer favourably.

The vices of any class are never to be imputed with the full force of disgraces to individuals. The vices of a class must evidently, from their extent, arise from some overpowering influences, under whose operation individuals should be respectfully compassionated, while the morbid influences are condemned. The

American clergy are the most backward and timid class in the society in which they live; self-exiled from the great moral questions of the time; the least informed with true knowledge; the least efficient in virtuous action; the least conscious of that christian and republican freedom which, as the native atmosphere of piety and holiness, it is their prime duty to cherish and diffuse. The proximate causes of their degeneracy in this respect are easily recognised.

It is not merely that the living of the clergy depends on the opinion of those whom they serve. To all but the far and clear-sighted it appears that the usefulness of their function does so. Ordinarily men may be excused for a willingness to seize on the precept about following after the things that make for peace, without too close an inquiry into the nature of that peace. Such a tendency may be excused, but not praised, in ordinary men. It must be blamed in all pastors who believe that they have grasped purer than ordinary principles of gospel freedom.

The first great mischief which arises from the disinclination of the clergy to bring what may be disturbing questions before their people is that they themselves inevitably undergo a perversion of views about the nature of their pastoral office. To take the most striking instance now presented in the United States. The clergy have not yet begun to stir upon the Anti-Slavery question. A very few Presbyterian clergymen have nobly risked everything for it; some being members of Abolition societies; and some professors in the Oberlin Institute and its branches, where all prejudice of colour is discountenanced. But the bulk of the Presbyterian clergy are as fierce as the slave-holders against the abolitionists. I believe they would not object to have Mr. Breckinridge[2] considered a sample of their body. The episcopalian clergy are generally silent on the subject of Human Rights, or give their influence against the Abolitionists. Not to go over the whole list of denominations, it is sufficient to mention that the ministers generally are understood to be opposed to abolition, from the circumstances of their silence in the pulpit, their conversation in society, and the conduct of those who are most under their influence. I pass on to

the Unitarians, the religious body with which I am best acquainted, from my being a Unitarian myself. The Unitarians
believe that they are not liable to many superstitions which cramp
the minds and actions of other religionists. They profess a religion
of greater freedom; and declare that Christianity, as they see it,
has an affinity with all that is free, genial, intrepid, and true in
the human mind; and that it is meant to be carried out into every
social arrangement, every speculation of thought, every act of
the life. Clergymen who preach this live in a crisis when a
tremendous conflict of principles is taking place. On one side is
the oppressor, struggling to keep his power for the sake of his
gold; and with him the mercenary, the faithlessly timid, the
ambitious, and the weak. On the other side are the friends of the
slave; and with them those who, without possibility of recompense, are sacrificing their reputations, their fortunes, their quiet,
and risking their lives, for the principle of freedom. What are the
Unitarian clergy doing amidst this war which admits of neither
peace nor truce, but which must end in the subjugation of the
principle of freedom, or of oppression?

I believe Mr. May[3] had the honour of being the first Unitarian
pastor who sided with the right. Whether he has sacrificed to his
intrepidity one christian grace; whether he has lost one charm of
his piety, gentleness, and charity, amidst the trials of insult which
he has had to undergo, I dare appeal to his worst enemy. Instead
of this, his devotion to a most difficult duty has called forth in
him a force of character, a strength of reason, of which his best
friends were before unaware. It filled me with shame for the
weakness of men, in their noblest offices, to hear the insolent
compassion with which some of his priestly brethren spoke of a
man whom they have not light and courage enough to follow
through the thickets and deserts of duty, and upon whom they
therefore bestow their scornful pity from out of their shady
bowers of complacency. Dr. Follen[4] came next: and there is
nothing in his power that he has not done and sacrificed in
identifying himself with the cause of emancipation. I heard him,
in a perilous time, pray in church for the "miserable, degraded,

insulted slave; in chains of iron, and chains of gold." This is not the place in which to exhibit what his sacrifices have really been. Dr. Channing's[5] later services are well known. I know of two more of the Unitarian clergy who have made an open and dangerous avowal of the right; and of one or two who have in private resisted wrong in the cause. But this is all. As a body they must, though disapproving slavery, be ranked as the enemies of the abolitionists. Some have pleaded to me that it is a distasteful subject. Some think it sufficient that they can see faults in individual abolitionists. Some say that their pulpits are the property of their people, who are not therefore to have their minds disturbed by what they hear thence. Some say that the question is no business of theirs. Some urge that they should be turned out of their pulpits before the next Sunday, if they touched upon Human Rights. Some think the subject not spiritual enough. The greater number excuse themselves on the ground of a doctrine which, I cannot but think, has grown out of the circumstances; that the duty of the clergy is to decide on how much truth the people can bear, and to administer it accordingly. So, while society is going through the greatest of moral revolutions, casting out its most vicious anomaly, and bringing its Christianity into its politics and its social conduct, the clergy, even the Unitarian clergy, are some pitying and some ridiculing the apostles of the revolution; preaching spiritualism, learning, speculation; advocating third- and fourth-rate objects of human exertion and amelioration, and leaving it to the laity to carry out the first and pressing moral reform of the age. They are blind to their noble mission of enlightening and guiding the moral sentiment of society in its greatest crisis. They not only decline aiding the cause in week-days by deed or pen, or spoken words; but they agree in private to avoid the subject of Human Rights in the pulpit till the crisis be past. No one asks them to harrow the feelings of their hearers by sermons on slavery: but they avoid offering those christian principles of faith and liberty with which slavery cannot co-exist.

Seeing what I have seen, I can come to no other conclusion

than that the most guilty class of the community in regard to the slavery question at present is, not the slave-holding, nor even the mercantile, but the clerical: the most guilty, because not only are they not blinded by life-long custom and prejudice, nor by pecuniary interest, but they profess to spend their lives in the study of moral relations, and have pledged themselves to declare the whole counsel of God. Whenever the day comes for the right principle to be established, let them not dare to glory in the glory of their country. Now, in its martyr-age, they shrink from being confessors. It will not be for them to march in to the triumph with the "glorious army." Yet, if the clergy of America follow the example of other rear-guards of society, they will be the first to glory in the reformation which they have done their utmost to retard.

The fearful and disgraceful mistake about the true nature of the clerical office—the supposition that it consists in adapting the truth to the minds of the hearers—is already producing its effect in thinning the churches, and impelling the people to find an administration of religion better suited to their need. The want of faith in other men and in principles, and the superabundant faith in themselves, shown in this notion of pastoral duty (which has been actually preached, as well as pleaded in private), are so conspicuous as to need no further exposure. The history of priesthoods may be referred to as an exhibition of its consequences. I was struck at first with an advocacy of Ordinances among some of the Unitarian clergy, which I was confident must go beyond their own belief. I was told that a great point was made of them (not as observances but as ordinances) because the public mind required them. I saw a minister using vehement and unaccustomed action (of course wholly inappropriate) in a pulpit not his own; and was told that that set of people required plenty of action to be assured the preacher was in earnest. I was told that when prejudices and interests have gathered round any point of morals, truth ceases to be truth, and it becomes a minister's duty to avoid the topic altogether. The consequences may be anticipated. "What do you think, sir, the people will do, as they discover the backwardness of their clergy?" I heard a minister of one sect say to a minister of another. "I think, sir, they will soon require a better clergy," was the reply. The people are requiring a better clergy. Even in Boston, so far behind the country as that city is, a notable change has already taken place. A strong man, full of enlarged sympathies, has not only discerned the wants of the time, but set himself to do what one man may to supply them. He invites to worship those who think and feel with him, as to what their communion with the Father must be, to sustain their principles and their cheer in this trying time. A multitude flocks round him; the earnest spirits of the city and the day, whose full hearts and worn spirits can find little ease and refreshment amidst the abstract and inappropriate services of ministers who give them truth as they judge they can receive it. Nothing but the whole truth will satisfy those who are living and dying for it. The rising up of this new church in Boston is an eloquent sign of the times.

An extraordinary revelation of the state of the case between the clergy and the people was made to me, most unconsciously, by a minister who, by the way, acknowledges that he avoids, on principle, preaching on the subjects which interest him most: he thinks he serves his people best by carrying into the pulpit subjects of secondary interest to himself. This gentleman, shocked with the tidings of some social tyranny on the anti-slavery question, exclaimed, "Such a revelation of the state of people's minds as this, is enough to make one leave one's pulpit, and set to work to mend society." What a volume do these few words disclose as to the relation of the clergy to the people and the time!

What the effect would be of the clergy carrying religion into what is most practically important, and therefore most interesting, is shown as often as opportunity occurs; which is all too seldom. When Dr. Channing dropped, in a sermon last winter, that legislatures as well as individuals were bound to do the will of God, every head in the church was raised or turned; every eye waited upon him. When another minister preached on being "alone," and showed how the noblest benefactors of the race, the truest servants of God, must, in striking out into new regions of thought and action, pass beyond the circle of common human sympathies, and suffer accordingly, many a stout heart melted into tears; many a rigid face crimsoned with emotion; and the sermon was repeated and referred to, far and near, under the name of "the Garrison sermon," a name given to it, not by the preacher, but by the consciences of some and the sympathies of others. Contrast with such an effect as this the influence of preaching, irrelevant to minds and seasons. If such sayings are admired or admitted at the moment, they are soon forgotten, or remembered only in the general. "Don't you think," said a gentleman to me, "that sermons are sadly useless things for the most part?—admonitions strung like bird's eggs on a string; so that they tell pretty much the same, backwards or forwards, one way or another."

It appears to me that the one thing in which the clergy of every kind are fatally deficient is faith: that faith which would lead them, first, to appropriate all truth, fearlessly and unconditionally; and then to give it as freely as they have received it. They are fond of apostolic authority. What would Paul's ministry have been if he had preached on everything but idolatry at Ephesus, and licentiousness at Corinth? There were people whose silver shrines, whose prejudices, whose false moral principles were in danger. There were people who were as unconscious of the depth of their sin as the oppressors of the Negro at the present day. How would Paul have then finished his course? If he had stopped short from the expediency of not dividing a household against itself, in case such should be the consequence of giving true principles to the air; if, dreading to break up the false peace of successful lucre and overbearing profligacy, he had confined himself to speculations like those with which he won the ear of the Athenians, carefully avoiding all allusions to Diana at Ephesus, and to temperance and judgment to come at Corinth, what kind of an apostle would he have been? Very like the American christian clergy of the nineteenth century.

The next great mischief that arises from the fear of opinion which makes the clergy keep aloof from the stirring questions of the time, is that they are deprived of that influence (the highest kind of all) that men exert by their individual characters and convictions. Their character is comparatively uninfluential from its being supposed professional; and their convictions, because they are concluded to be formed from imperfect materials. A clergyman's opinions on politics, and on other affairs of active life in which morals are most implicated, are attended to precisely in proportion as he is secular in his habits and pursuits. A minister preached, a few years ago, against discount, and high prices in times of scarcity. The merchants of his flock went away laughing: and the pastor has never got over it. The merchants speak of him as a very holy man, and esteem his services highly for keeping their wives, children, and domestics in strict religious order: but in preaching to themselves he has been preaching to the winds ever since that day. A liberal-minded, religious father of a family said to me, "Take care how you receive the uncorroborated statements of clergymen about that" (a matter of social fact); "they know nothing about it. They are not likely to know anything about it." "Why?" "Because there is nobody to tell them. You know the clergy are looked upon by all grown men as a sort of people between men and women." In a republic, where politics afford the discipline and means of expression of every man's morals, the clergy withdraw from, not only all party movements, but all political interests. Some barely vote: others do not even do this. Their plea is, as usual, that public opinion will not bear that the clergy should be upon the same footing as to worldly affairs as others. If this be true, public opinion should not be allowed to dictate their private duty to the moral teachers of society. A clergyman should discharge the duties of a citizen all the more faithfully for the need which the public thus show themselves to be in of his example. But, if it be true, whence arises the objection of the public to the clergy discharging the responsibilities of citizens, but from the popular belief that they are unfitted for it? If the democracy see that the clergy are almost all federalists, and the federalist merchants and

lawyers consider the clergy so little fit for common affairs as to
call them a set of people between men and women, it is easy to
see whence arises the dislike to their taking part in politics; if
indeed the dislike really exists. The statement should not, however, be taken on the word of the clergy alone; for they are very
apt to think that the people cannot yet bear many things in which
the flocks have already outstripped their pastors.

A third great mischief from the isolation of the clergy is that,
while it deprives them of the highest kind of influence which is
the prerogative of manhood, it gives them a lower kind: an
influence as strong as it is pernicious to others, and dangerous to
themselves; an influence confined to the weak members of society;
women and superstitious men. By such they are called "faithful
guardians." Guardians of what? A healthy person may guard a
sick one; a sane man may guard a lunatic; a grown person may
guard a child; and, for social purposes, an appointed watch may
guard a criminal. But how can any man guard his equal in
spiritual matters, the most absolutely individual of all? How can
any man come between another's soul and the infinite to which it
tends? If it is said that they are guardians of truth, and not of
conscience, they may be asked for their warrant. God has given
his truth for all. Each is to lay hold of what he can receive of it;
and he sins if he devolves upon an other the guardianship of
what is given him for himself. As to the fitness of the clergy to
be guardians, it is enough to mention what I know: that there is
infidelity within the walls of their churches of which they do
not dream; and profligacy among their flocks of which they will
be the last to hear. Even in matters which are esteemed their
peculiar business, the state of faith and morals, they are more in
the dark than any other persons in society. Some of the most
religious and moral persons in the community are among those
who never enter their churches; while among the company who
sit at the feet of the pastor while he refines upon abstractions,
and builds a moral structure upon imperfect principles, or upon
metaphysical impossibilities, there are some in whom the very
capacity of stedfast belief has been cruelly destroyed; some who

hide loose morals under a strict profession of religion; and some if possible more lost still, who have arrived at making their religion co-exist with their profligacy. Is there not here something like the blind leading the blind?

Over those who consider the clergy "faithful guardians," their influence, as far as it is professional, is bad; as far as it is that of friendship or acquaintanceship, it is according to the characters of the men. I am disposed to think ill of the effects of the practice of parochial visiting, except in cases of poor and afflicted persons, who have little other resource of human sympathy. I cannot enlarge upon the disagreeable subject of the devotion of the ladies to the clergy. I believe there is no liberal-minded minister who does not see, and too sensibly feel, the evil of women being driven back upon religion as a resource against vacuity; and of their being a professional class to administer it. Some of the most sensible and religious elderly women I know in America speak, with a strength which evinces strong conviction, of the mischief to their sex of ministers entering the profession young and poor, and with a great enthusiasm for parochial visiting. There is no very wide difference between the auricular confession of the catholic church, and the spiritual confidence reposed in ministers the most devoted to visiting their flocks. Enough may be seen in the religious periodicals of America about the help women give to young ministers by the needle, by raising subscriptions, and by more toilsome labours than they should be allowed to undergo in such a cause. If young men cannot earn with their own hands the means of finishing their education, and providing themselves with food and clothing, without the help of women, they may safely conclude that their vocation is to get their bread first; whether or not it may be to preach afterwards. But this kind of dependence is wholly unnecessary. There is more provision made for the clergy than there are clergy to use it.

A young clergyman came home, one day, and complained to me that some of his parochial visiting afflicted him much. He had been visiting and exhorting a mother who had lost her infant; a sorrow which he always found he could not reach. The mourner had sat still, and heard all he had to say: but his impression was that he had not met any of her feelings; that he had done nothing but harm. How should it be otherwise? What should he know of the grief of a mother for her infant? He was sent for, as a kind of charmer, to charm away the heart's pain. Such pain is not sent to be charmed away. It could be made more endurable only by sympathy, of all outward aids: and sympathy, of necessity, he had none; but only a timid pain with which to aggravate hers. It was natural that he should do nothing but harm.

My final impression is that religion is best administered in America by the personal character of the most virtuous members of society, out of the theological profession: and next, by the acts and preachings of the members of that profession who are the most secular in their habits of mind and life. The exclusively clerical are the worst enemies of Christianity, except the vicious.

The fault is not in the Voluntary System; for the case is equally bad on both sides the Atlantic; and an Establishment like the English does little more than superadd the danger of a careless, ambitious, worldly clergy,* in the richer priests of the church, and an overworked and ill-recompensed set of working clergy. The evil lies in a superstition which no establishment can ever obviate; in the superstition, to use the words of an American clergyman, "of believing that religion is something else than goodness." From this it arises than an ecclesiastical profession still exists; not for the study of theological science (which is quite reasonable), but for the dispensing of goodness. From this it arises that ecclesiastical goodness is practically separated from active personal and social goodness. From this it arises that the yeomanry of America, those who are ever in the presence of God's high priest, Nature, and out of the worldly competitions of a society sophisticated with superstition, are perpetually in advance of the rest of the community on the great moral questions of the time, while the clergy are in the rear.

* It is amusing to see how our aristocratic and ecclesiastical institutions strike simple republicans. I was asked whether the English Bishops were not a necessary intermediate aristocracy between the Lords and the Commons.

What must be done? The machinery of administration must be changed. The people have been brought up to suppose that they saw Christianity in their ministers. The first consequence of this mistake was that Christianity was extensively misunderstood; as it still is. The trying moral conflicts of the time are acting as a test. The people are rapidly discovering that the supposed faithful mirror is a grossly refracting medium; and the blessed consequence will be that they will look at the object for themselves, declining any medium at all. The clerical profession is too hard and too perilous a one, too little justifiable on the ground of principle, too much opposed to the spirit of the gospel, to outlive long the individual research into religion to which the faults of the clergy are daily impelling the people.

To what then must we meantime trust for religion? To the administration of God, and the heart of man. Has not God his own ways, unlike our ways, of teaching when man misteaches? It is worth travelling in the wild west, away from churches and priests, to see how religion springs up in the pleasant woods, and is nourished by the winds and the star-light. The child on the grass is not alone listening for God's tramp on the floor of his creation. We are all children, ever so listening. Impulses of religion arise wherever there is life and society; whenever hope is rebuked, and fear relieved; wherever there is love to be cherished, and age and childhood to be guarded. If it be true, as my friend and I speculated, that religious sensibility is best awakened by the spectacle of the beauty of holiness, religion is everywhere safe; for this beauty is as prevalent, more or less perceptibly, as the light of human eyes. It is safe as long as the gospel history is extant. The beauty of holiness is there so resplendent that, to those who look upon it with their own eyes, it seems inconceivable that, if it were once brought unveiled before the minds of men, every one would not adopt it into his reason and his affections from that hour. It has been reorganising and vivifying society from the day of its advent. It is carrying on this very work now in the New World. The institutions of America are, as I have said, planted down deep into Christianity. Its spirit must make an effectual pilgrimage through a society, of which it may be called a native; and no mistrust of its influences can for ever intercept that spirit in its mission of denouncing anomalies, exposing hypocrisy, rebuking faithlessness, raising and communing with the outcast, and driving out sordidness from the circuit of this, the most glorious temple of society that has ever yet been reared. The community will be christian as sure as democracy is christian.

NOTES

[1] A full discussion of anti-Catholic sentiment in this period will be found in Ray Allen Billington, *The Protestant Crusade* (Chicago: Quadrangle Books, 1964).

[2] Robert Jefferson Breckinridge (1800–1871) was a son of Thomas Jefferson's attorney general, John Breckinridge (1760–1806), and a prominent Presbyterian clergyman of his day. At the time of Harriet Martineau's visit he was pastor of the Second Presbyterian Church in Baltimore. Her reference here is apparently to the moderation which characterized his antislavery views.

[3] Probably Samuel Joseph May (1797–1871), who served Unitarian congregations in Connecticut, Massachusetts, and New York. May, a good friend and early supporter of William Lloyd Garrison, was prominent in antislavery activities throughout the pre-Civil War era.

[4] Charles Follen (1796–1840) was born and educated in Germany, but was forced to leave his homeland because of his outspoken liberalism. After coming to America in 1824, he lectured on law and philosophy at Harvard, but lost his position there because of his abolitionist views.

[5] William Ellery Channing (1780–1842) was the chief Unitarian spokesman of his day. His liberal theology and sensitive social conscience had a formative influence upon Unitarianism and upon American social and religious thought generally.

14

George Combe

George Combe (1788–1858) was well known in Europe and America as an apostle of phrenology, a pseudo-science which achieved a certain degree of respectability in the early nineteenth century. He was born and educated in Edinburgh, where, as a young man, he attended a series of lectures given by Johann Gaspar Spurzheim, a student and disciple of Franz Gall, the Viennese physician who had originated phrenology. Combe went to Paris to study with Spurzheim and then returned to Edinburgh, where he lectured on phrenology, founded a society and a journal for the propagation of his views, and in 1828 published *The Constitution of Man*. This work contains the fullest statement of his doctrines, and according to John Davies is "the best known and most inspirational of all phrenological books."[1]

The book from which the following is taken resulted from an American lecture tour that started in 1838 and ended in 1840. Though accused of atheism in England and Scotland because of the materialistic tendencies of phrenology, Combe appears to have been an earnest if latitudinarian theist. He was persistently curious about religious affairs in America, especially the material and spiritual conditions of the churches under the voluntary system.

[*from* NOTES ON THE UNITED STATES]

I CONVERSED to-day with a gentleman of great acuteness and experience, who has observed the progress of manners in New England, for upwards of half a century. He mentioned, that within that time there has been a great diminution in convivial drinking among the higher classes, independently of the influence of temperance societies, and that at dinner, the gentlemen drink much less wine. I have already had occasion to remark the exemplary temperance in this respect of the gentlemen in the first class of society here. Dinner is served at three o'clock, a few glasses of wine are taken, conversation proceeds with spirit, and the entertainment terminates by a cup of coffee brought to the table about six o'clock. In many instances, the gentlemen retire to the drawing-room, and join the ladies an hour earlier. Some families, who have been much in Europe, dine at six o'clock, and entertain in the English style; but this is by no means common.

My friend continued to say, that their Voluntary Church system has led to the multiplication of churches even to excess, and to inadequate provision for the ministers, and has also, in some instances, occasioned animosities among the people. The dependence of the clergy on their hearers has led some of them to study their humours, and to preach fanatical doctrines for the sake of excitement, rather than to follow the dictates of their own understandings. He has observed, however, that from there being among the sects no artificial distinctions created by the law, these animosities speedily subside, and that there is a constant tendency in the public mind to correct its own errors. The usual time now occupied by divine service in Boston, is an hour or an hour and a quarter. The morning service begins at half-past ten, and ends at a quarter before twelve. The afternoon service begins at three. The time employed in public worship has been much shortened within his recollection. There is a growing disposition in the people to subject religion to the examination of reason; and opinion is, in some instances, passing even beyond Unitarianism. Still Calvinism, in its purest forms, is extensively professed by the people. . . .

On the 4th of August 1838, Lord Brougham[2] is reported to have stated, in his place in Parliament, that the Voluntary Church system has not answered in America. I have endeavoured, by inquiries made of persons whom I conceived likely to be well-informed, to discover what inconveniences have attended it. The following circumstances have been mentioned to me as evils. The congregations, it is said, are adopting the practice of engaging their ministers for only three, five, or seven years, and then turning them adrift, if they are not satisfied. In the villages, also, there are so many churches that some of them languish.

I asked whether the congregations act capriciously in dismissing their pastor, at the end of the stipulated engagement; and have been told that they do not intentionally act capriciously; but that as the minister with whose services they have dispensed is occasionally found to be highly acceptable to a different congregation, this charge is made against them with a shew of reason by those who differ from them in opinion.

It appears to me that this system of change, if generally adopted, would be attended with advantages, especially in the present condition of clerical instruction. Within less than seven years, most clergymen have exhausted their whole stock of ideas in preaching and ministering to their people, and although they continue their labours for forty years longer, they do not communicate a new view. By changing pastors, fresh minds would be brought to operate on the flocks, and a greater degree of energy would pervade the service. If rotation in churches prevailed, no minister of talent and industry would lack employment; for the vacancy made by the removal of one would be supplied by the call of another to fill his place.

In regard to the multiplication of churches, I remarked that one of Dr. Chalmers[3] arguments in favour of an Establishment is that men have no appetite for religion, and that, if left to themselves, the will neither build churches, nor endow pastors, but prefer remaining in heathenism. Here, however, we are assured that, under the Voluntary system, "church extension" goes on too rapidly, and that pastors and churches are more numerous than flocks!

One instance, however, was mentioned to me of a clergyman suffering annoyance from a fearless discharge of his duty. The Rev. John Pierpont,[4] a Unitarian pastor, a man of great talent, and of the purest morals, has preached too strongly against in-temperance, and taken too active a part in the temperance cause, to suit the taste of his congregation, a large proportion of whom are distillers and retailers of spirituous liquors. These have taken offence, and on a recent vote to decide whether his letter in explanation of his conduct was satisfactory or not, fifty-eight proprietors of pews voted "yea," and forty-four "nay." This vote is an approval by a majority, and he continues his ministerial functions. This case shews, however, that under the Voluntary system a minister is not necessarily the slave of his congregation, and that if instances to the contrary occur, the cause of them must be sought in the weakness of the individual who yields because he does not feel that self-sustaining power and independ-ence which high endowments confer.

In answering my inquiries into their church affairs, some of my Boston friends asked me what objections were urged in Britain against the system of legal establishments for the support of reli-gion. I mentioned a few: The established clergy in England and Scotland support unalterable articles of faith declared by ancient acts of Parliament to be true interpretations of the will of God, and important to salvation: They expel from their livings every one of their own number who presumes to express doubts of the infallible truths of any of these doctrines: They invite their flocks to search the Scriptures, to try all things, and to hold fast that which is good; but if, in following this advice, the flocks chance to arrive at conclusions different from those sanctioned by act of Parliament, they are charged with heresy, denied church privi-leges, and in private are stigmatized as "bad men." These articles and "Confessions of Faith," moreover, were framed at the very dawn of civilization, when the arts and sciences, and the philoso-phy of the human mind, scarcely existed. Consequently some of the doctrines contained in them stand in direct contradiction to natural truth, while the entire scheme of theology which they propound is widely different from that which an extensive knowl-edge of mental and physical science applied to the interpretation of Scripture in the present day would probably dictate. The professors of these doctrines have the command of the parish schools, and of the universities, and to the extent of their ability they infuse their opinions into each generation as it comes on the stage: But mind cannot be arrested in its progress. Providence bestows on some individuals superior endowments of the moral and intellectual faculties, which lead their possessors into doubt on some points in spite of themselves. But those who are thus gifted have a choice only between two evils; either to renounce their livings and depart into the wilderness of voluntaryism, as outcasts from the fold of the faithful, or to practise hypocrisy. The latter is sometimes preferred, although not without inward struggles. Some of these individuals may be heard praying publicly against "a wicked spirit of unbelief," which is constantly besetting them, and which is probably nothing; but the natural operation of their own superior faculties spontaneously suggesting truth, and quietly whispering that some of the dogmas they teach are erroneous. Other individuals, in whom secretiveness is large, and conscientiousness deficient, feel quite at home in the regions of hypocrisy, and enjoy their legal salaries undisturbed by inward visitations. Far from being the advocates of natural science and liberal education, many of the clergy oppose both, and insist that their peculiar articles of faith shall be combined with all public instruction at the expense of the State. They are placed in a false position also in relation to the enlightened portion of the laity, who, while they ostensibly adhere to the parliamentary articles of faith, privately disbelieve them, and, in consequence, while they accord an outward homage to the church, never lose an opportunity to thwart the schemes and defeat the views of the clergy. Conventional hypocrisy, likewise, is the refuge of the philosophers under the dominion of an established church. There is a tacit convention of mutual forbearance between them and the clergy: The clergy make no inquiries into their orthodoxy, and, in return, they leave the clergy to guide the masses in their own paths. The general effect of the system is to chain up the intellect, and paralyze the moral sentiments of the best minds in the highest department of human thought—theological and moral science.

It is objected also to legal establishments for the support of religion, that their natural tendency is to render the clergy indolent and negligent. The churches of England and Ireland present numerous examples of clergymen who, although enjoying rich endowments, are never seen by their flocks. Indifference in the pastors is the parent of indifference and formality in the people. The "pride, pomp, and circumstance" of a state-establishment produce supercilious feelings in the favoured clergy towards the pastors of all other sects; and the possession of legal power incites them to outrage the rights of conscience, by levying taxes from dissenters for the support of opinions which they disavow.

In the foregoing remarks on the voluntary and the legal systems, the abuses or worst features of both are stated and compared; while in the discussions which generally take place on these topics, all that is good in the one is contrasted with all that is bad in the other, a very unfair mode of treating the merits of either. There is much of good found in both. In point of fact, an able and conscientious minister in the voluntary church, unless in very peculiar circumstances, like those of Mr. Pierpont, soon rivets himself in the esteem and affections of his people, and is cherished by them for life; while a clergyman of the same character in the established church is equally beloved and respected by his flock. Good, able, and active men are safe and independent in both, in so far as mere emolument is concerned; but the establishment is a paradise, while the voluntary church is a howling wilderness, for incapacity, indolence, folly, dishonesty, and the minor vices. The chief difference in the case of good and able men is, that, under the voluntary system, an individual of superior piety, talents, and attainments has it in his power to carry forward his flock to higher and purer views of Christianity, in proportion as these open up to his own mind (and he often does so in the United States); while his equal in the established church is tied down by the parliamentary articles of belief; he is the slave of them, and of his weaker brethren, who are ever ready to defend the bulwarks of ignorance and indolence under the guise of maintaining the purity of the faith, and to enforce the law of expulsion against any more gifted member, who would venture to remove one stone of the legal edifice. In America, as I formerly mentioned, the whole statute law of each State is revised every ten years; obsolete and repealed acts are omitted; altered statutes are remodelled into a connected and consistent form, and the whole laws are brought to harmonize, as much as possible, with the existing condition of the people: But the principles of infallibility and immutability are inherent in the nature of an established church. The state of human knowledge may change, opinion may change, political institutions may change, and generation may give way to generation, but the articles of faith ratified and approved of by act of Parliament never vary! . . .

The following anecdote is *not* an old Joe Miller. I relate it because, while it illustrates the kindly feeling which reigns among the members of a sect towards each other, it shews how this amiable trait of character may be taken advantage of by rogues. A bookseller, a native of Germany, came from England, settled in one of the large American cities, and began business in a moderate way. He had a stock of neatly printed bibles which he was anxious to dispose of. After he had been established for some time, he called on an old-established citizen, and told him that he thought of joining one of the religious bodies of the town, and wished to know which of them was the most influential. His friend imagined that he was in joke, and said that there was a simple way of solving that question. He took up the *directory* and shewed the inquiring bookseller the lists of the directors of all the public institutions. He desired him to write down their names, and he would tell him what sects they belonged to. The bookseller accordingly folded his paper for columns, and wrote on the heads of them, "Presbyterian," "Methodist," "Catholic," "Quaker," "Baptist," "Unitarian," "Universalist," "Jew," &c., and under these heads entered the names of the directors of the institutions, according to the information of his friend. The result was a clear demonstration that the "Presbyterians" were by far the most numerous and powerful sect in the public institutions, whence the inference was drawn that in all probability they would be the most influential in the general affairs of the city.

He thanked the gentleman (who still believed that it was a jest) and departed. But it was neither a joke nor a mistake. The bookseller found out which was the wealthiest Presbyterian congregation, offered to join them, and presented a handsome gift to the church, and neatly bound copies of his bible to the minister and elders. He was admitted a member, was widely praised among the congregation, sold all his bibles, obtained extensive credit, had a large store and an ample trade, and might have done well. But, like too many others, he speculated and ruined himself. At his bankruptcy, the rich men of the congregation were his creditors, one to the extent of $20,000, another of $15,000, another of $10,000, and so forth, every man according to his means!

This is no uncommon occurrence in other countries, and it is proof of the real Christian spirit of the individuals who are thus cheated. Having entire confidence in the efficacy of their own faith to regenerate the human mind, and being perfectly sincere themselves, they do not suspect the roguery of others. In reference to an individual of a character very similar to this, who had come from Scotland, I was asked, "How do you reconcile the strange and striking discrepancy between the religious professions and the commercial reputation of your countryman Mr. A. B.?" The explanation which I offered, and which I knew to be supported by facts, was, that in the class of persons to which Mr. A. B. belongs, the organs of Acquisitiveness, Secretiveness, and Veneration, are *plus*, and those of Conscientiousness *minus*. The large Veneration gives them a strong interest in religious worship, and to this extent their professions are sincere. It reveals to them also the power of this sentiment in other minds. Then large Secretiveness and deficient Conscientiousness, when combined with acute intellect, render them apt at swindling and deceit; and thus accomplished, they are tempted to employ the religious feeling as a means of gratifying their Acquisitiveness. . . .

Should British Dissenting Clergymen Emigrate to America? This question is often put by letters to the American clergy, and personally to individuals who have visited the United States. My advice to them is to let well alone, and stay in their own country, if they can obtain a decent livelihood. A clergyman must be born and "reared" in the United States to fit him for his situation and duties. The deficiency of domestic service, the high rents and exorbitant price of most manufactured and imported articles in the cities, the limited extent of social habits, the arduous labour, the strict surveillance exercised by society over official persons, and the overwhelming force of public opinion—render the United States no paradise to well educated men accustomed to social life in Britain. . . .

I perceive that the liberality of the different sects towards each other increases in proportion to the number and standing in society of the adherents of each. In Boston, the Unitarians are numerous, and belong to the first class. There I could discover no ostensible prejudice against them. The Governor of the State and the Secretary of State were Unitarians; and among the magistrates and school directors, they were found co-operating with Calvinists and men of other sects in all public duties, without dissension or disrespect on any side. In New York, where the Unitarians have only two congregations, and are of comparatively recent origin, the prejudices entertained against them by the orthodox sects are stronger; and in Philadelphia, where they are still more recent, and have only one church, the dislike of them is still more conspicuously manifested. It has been remarked that sectarian hatred increases in proportion as the differences in opinion between the partisans diminish. The animosity, for instance, expressed by Calvinists against Jews is far less than that manifested against Unitarians.*

---

* In Scotland, where both the Church and the Dissenters are almost all Calvinists, intolerance reaches its maximum; and the religious public are far from manifesting that liberal and Christian spirit which, while it holds fast by that which it regards as right, recognises its own fallibility, and admits the privilege of other men to do the same, without offering disparagement to their characters in thought, word, or deed.

NOTES

[1] John D. Davies, *Phrenology: Fad and Science* (New Haven: Yale University Press, 1955), p. 14.

[2] Henry Peter Brougham (1778–1868), Scottish jurist and member of the House of Lords, had been instrumental in the success of the Reform Bill in 1831.

[3] Thomas Chalmers (1780–1847), Scottish clergyman and theologian, was best known in America for his *Institutes of Theology*.

[4] John Pierpont (1785–1866) was a Unitarian minister in Boston from 1819 to 1845. John Pierpont Morgan, the financier, was his grandson.

15

Philip Schaff

In 1843 representatives of the Eastern Synod of the German Reformed Church went to Europe to find a well-trained German scholar to teach theology at their newly established seminary at Mercersburg, Pennsylvania. They succeeded in hiring Philip Schaff (1819–1893), a brilliant young man who had come from obscure poverty in Switzerland to study at Tübingen, at Halle, and finally at the University of Berlin, where he received the doctorate in 1841, at the age of twenty-two. Schaff survived a charge of heresy—the initial response to his German theological training—to become the intellectual leader of the German-American church. He and John Williamson Nevin comprised the entire faculty of Mercersburg and, in addition, edited the *Mercersburg Review*. Schaff produced works on church history, including a seven-volume *History of the Christian Church*, composed a liturgy for the American church, and edited a *commentary* and the *Religious Encyclopaedia*. In 1865 he moved to New York, joined the faculty of Union Seminary, participated in such early efforts at church unity as the Evangelical Alliance, and continued to pursue his scholarly tasks.

Few men have been so well qualified to interpret American Christianity in the nineteenth century. Schaff first did so in 1853, when he made his first return trip to Germany. He gave two lectures, one in Berlin and one in Frankfort, that were translated and published together in 1855 as *America: A Sketch of its Political, Social, and Religious Character*. Expected to detail the sad plight into which American Protestantism had fallen, Schaff produced instead a sensitive appraisal informed by his understanding of church history and his new-found sympathy with the voluntary system.

[*from* AMERICA]

IT is a vast advantage to that country itself, and one may say to the whole world, that the United States were first settled in great part from religious motives; that the first emigrants left the homes of their fathers for faith and conscience' sake, and thus at the outset stamped upon their new home the impress of positive Christianity, which now exerts a wholesome influence even on those later emigrants who have no religion at all.

The ecclesiastical character of America, however, is certainly very different from that of the Old World. Two points in particular require notice.

The first is this. While in Europe ecclesiastical institutions appear in historical connection with Catholicism, and even in evangelical countries, most of the city and village churches, the universities, and religious foundations, point to a mediaeval origin; in North America, on the contrary, every thing had a Protestant beginning, and the Catholic Church has come in afterwards as one sect among the others, and has always remained subordinate. In Europe, Protestantism has, so to speak, fallen heir to Catholicism; in America, Catholicism under the wing of Protestant toleration and freedom of conscience, has found an adopted home, and is everywhere surrounded by purely Protestant institutions. True, the colony of Maryland, planted by the Catholic Lord Baltimore, was one of the earliest settlements of North America. But, in the first place, even this was by no means specifically Roman. It was founded expressly on the thoroughly anti-Roman, and essentially Protestant, principles of religious toleration. And then, again, it never had any specific influence on the character of the country; for even the prominent position of the city of Baltimore, as the American metropolis of the Roman Church, is of much later date. Far more important and influential were the settlements of the Puritans in New England, the Episcopalians in Virginia, the Quakers in Pennsylvania, the Dutch in New York, in the course of the seventeenth century, the Presbyterians from Scotland and

North Ireland, and the German Lutherans and Reformed from the Palatinate, in the first half of the eighteenth. These have given the country its spirit and character. Its past course and present condition are unquestionably due mainly to the influence of Protestant principles. The Roman Church has attained social and political importance in the eastern and western States only within the last twenty years, chiefly in consequence of the vast Irish emigration; but it will never be able to control the doctrines of the New World, though it should increase a hundred fold.

Another peculiarity in the ecclesiastical condition of North America, connected with the Protestant origin and character of the country, is the separation of church and state. The infidel reproach, that had it not been for the power of the state, Christianity would have long ago died out; and the argument of Roman controversialists, that Protestantism could not stand without the support of princes and civil governments, both are practically refuted and utterly annihilated in the United States. The president and governors, the congress at Washington, and the state legislatures, have, as such, nothing to do with the church, and are by the Constitution expressly forbidden to interfere in its affairs. State officers have no other rights in the church, than their personal rights as members of particular denominations. The church, indeed, everywhere enjoys the protection of the laws for its property, and the exercise of its functions; but it manages its own affairs independently, and has also to depend for its resources entirely on voluntary contributions. As the state commits itself to no particular form of Christianity, there is of course also no civil requisition of baptism, confirmation, and communion. Religion is left to the free will of each individual, and the church has none but moral means of influencing the world.

This separation was by no means a sudden, abrupt event, occasioned, say, by the Revolution. The first settlers, indeed, had certainly no idea of such a thing; they proceeded rather on Old Testament theocratic principles, like Calvin, John Knox, the Scottish Presbyterians, and the English Puritans of the seventeenth century; regarding state and church as the two arms of one of the same divine will. In the colony of Massachusetts, the Puritans, in fact, founded a rigid Calvinistic state-church system. They made the civil franchise depend on membership in the church; and punished not only blasphemy and open infidelity, but even every departure from the publicly acknowledged code of Christian faith and practice as a political offense. In Boston, in the seventeenth century, even the Quakers, who certainly acted there in a very fanatical and grossly indecent way, were formally persecuted, publicly scourged, imprisoned, and banished; and, in Salem, of the same State, witches were burnt as accomplices of the devil. The last traces of this state-church system in New England were not obliterated till long after the American Revolution, and even to this day most of the States have laws for the observance of the Sabbath, monogamy, and other specifically Christian institutions. Thus the separation of the temporal and spiritual powers is by no means absolute. While New England had Congregationalism for its established religion, New York also had at first the Dutch Reformed, and afterwards the English Episcopal church, and Virginia, and some other Southern States, also the English Episcopal, for their establishments. With these the other forms of Christianity were tolerated either not at all, or under serious restrictions, as formerly the Dissenters were in England.

But on the other hand, there prevailed in other North American colonies from their foundation, therefore long before the Revolution of 1776, entire freedom of faith and conscience; as in Rhode Island, founded by the Baptist, Roger Williams, who was banished from Massachusetts for heresy, and thus set by bitter experience against religious intolerance; in Pennsylvania, which the Quaker, William Penn, originally designed as an asylum for his brethren in faith, but to which he soon invited also German Reformed and Lutherans from the Palatinate, guaranteeing equal rights to all, and leaving each to the guidance of the "inward light"; and, finally, in Maryland, founded by Lord Baltimore on the same basis of universal religious toleration.

After the American Revolution this posture of the State gradually became general. First, the legislature of Virginia, after the colony had separated from the mother-country, annulled the rights and privileges of the Episcopal establishment, and placed all the dissenting bodies on a perfectly equal footing with it in the eye of the law. Her example was followed by the other colonies, which had established churches. When Congress was organized at the close of the war, an article was placed in the Constitution, forbidding the enactment of laws about religion; and similar prohibitions are found in the constitutions of the several States.

We would by no means vindicate this separation of church and state as the perfect and final relation between the two. The kingdom of Christ is to penetrate and transform like leaven, all the relations of individual and national life. We much prefer this separation, however, to the territorial system and a police guardianship of the church, the Bride of the God-man, the free-born daughter of heaven; and we regard it as adapted to the present wants of America, and favorable to her religious interests. For it is by no means to be thought that the separation of church and state there is a renunciation of Christianity by the nation; like the separation of the state and the school from the church, and the civil equality of Atheism with Christianity, which some members of the abortive Frankfurt Parliament[1] were for introducing in Germany. It is not an annihilation of one factor, but only an amicable separation of the two in their spheres of outward operation; and thus equally the church's declaration of independence towards the state, and an emancipation of the state from bondage to a particular confession. The nation, therefore, is still Christian, though it refuses to be governed in this deepest concern of the mind and heart by the temporal power. In fact, under such circumstances, Christianity, as the free expression of personal conviction and of the national character, has even greater power over the mind, than when enjoined by civil laws and upheld by police regulations.

This appears practically in the strict observance of the Sabbath, the countless churches and religious schools, the zealous support of Bible and Tract societies, of domestic and foreign missions, the numerous revivals, the general attendance on divine worship, and the custom of family devotion—all expressions of the general Christian character of the people, in which the Americans are already in advance of most of the old Christian nations of Europe.

In fact, even the state, as such, to some extent officially recognizes Christianity. Congress appoints chaplains (mostly from the Episcopal, sometimes from the Presbyterian and the Methodist clergy) for itself, the army, and the navy. It opens every day's session with prayer, and holds public worship on the Sabbath in the Senate Chamber at Washington. The laws of the several States also contain strict prohibitions of blasphemy, atheism, Sabbath-breaking, polygamy, and other gross violations of general Christian morality.

Thus the separation is not fully carried out in practice, on account of the influence of Christianity on the popular mind. It is even quite possible that the two powers may still come into collision. The tolerance of the Americans has its limits and counterpoise in that religious fanaticism, to which they are much inclined. This may be seen in the expulsion of the Mormons, who so grossly offended the religious and moral sense of the people. Great political difficulties may arise, especially from the growth of the Roman church, which has been latterly aiming everywhere at political influence, and thus rousing the jealousy and opposition of the great Protestant majority. The Puritanic Americans see in Catholicism an ecclesiastical despotism, from which they fear also political despotism, so that its sway in the United States must be the death of Republican freedom. Thus the Catholic question has already come to be regarded by many as at the same time a political question, involving the existence of the Republic; and a religious war between Catholics and Protestants, though in the highest degree improbable, is still by no means an absolute impossibility; as, in fact, slight skirmishes have already occurred in the street fight between the two parties in Philadelphia in 1844, and the violent demolition of a Roman convent at Charlestown, Mass. The secret political party of the "Know-Nothings," which is just sweeping over the States with the rapidity of the whirlwind, but which, for this very reason, cannot last long in this particular form, is mainly directed against the influence of Romanism.

If, however, the great question of the relation of church and state be not by any means fully solved even in the United States, still the two powers are there at all events much more distant than in any other country.

The natural result of this arrangement is a general prevalence of freedom of conscience and religious faith, and of the voluntary principle, as it is called: that is, the promotion of every religious work by the free-will offerings of the people. The state, except in the few cases mentioned above, does nothing towards building churches, supporting ministers, founding theological seminaries, or aiding indigent students in preparation for the ministry. No taxes are laid for these objects; no one is compelled to contribute a farthing to them. What is done for them is far, indeed, from being always done from the purest motives—love to God and to religion—often from a certain sense of honor, and for all sorts of selfish by-ends; yet always from free impulses, without any outward coercion.

This duly considered, it is truly wonderful what a multitude of churches, ministers, colleges, theological seminaries, and benevolent institutions are there founded and maintained entirely by free-will offerings. In Berlin there are hardly forty churches for a population of four hundred and fifty thousand, of whom, in spite of all the union of church and state, only some thirty thousand attend public worship. In New York, to a population of six hundred thousand, there are over two hundred and fifty well-attended churches, some of them quite costly and splendid, especially on Broadway and Fifth Avenue. In the city of Brooklyn, across the East River, the number of churches is still larger in proportion to the population, and in the country towns and villages, especially in New England, the houses of worship average one to every thousand, or frequently even five hundred, souls. If these are not Gothic cathedrals, they are yet mostly decent, comfortable buildings, answering all the purposes of the congregation often even far better than the most imposing works of architecture. In every new city district, in every new settlement, one of the first things thought of is the building of a temple to the Lord, where the neighboring population may be regularly fed with the bread of life and encouraged to labor, order, obedience, and every good work. Suppose the state, in Germany, should suddenly withdraw its support from church and university, how many preachers and professors would be breadless, and how many auditories closed!

The voluntary system unquestionably has its great blemishes. It is connected with all sorts of petty drudgery, vexations, and troubles, unknown in well endowed Established Churches. Ministers and teachers, especially among the recent German emigrants in America, who have been accustomed to State provision for religion and education, have very much to suffer from the free system. They very often have to make begging tours for the erection of a church, and submit to innumerable other inconveniences for the good cause, till a congregation is brought into a proper course, and its members become practised in free giving.

But, on the other hand, the voluntary system calls forth a mass of individual activity and interest among the laity in ecclesiastical affairs, in the founding of new churches and congregations, colleges and seminaries, in home and foreign missions, and in the promotion of all forms of Christian philanthropy. We may here apply in a good sense our Lord's word: "Where the treasure is, there the heart will be also." The man who, without coercion, brings his regular offering for the maintenance of the church and the minister, has commonly much more interest in both, and in their prosperity he sees with pleasure the fruit of his own labor. The same is true of seminaries. All the congregations and synods are interested in the theological teacher, whom they support, and who trains ministers of the Word for them; while in Europe the people give themselves little or no trouble about the theological faculties.

It is commonly thought that this state of things necessarily involves an unworthy dependence of the minister on his congregation. But this is not usually the case. The Americans expect a minister to do his duty, and they most esteem that one who fearlessly and impartially declares the whole counsel of God, and presents the depravity of man and the threatenings of the Divine Word as faithfully as he does the comforting promises. Cases of ministers employed for a certain time, as hired servants, occur indeed occasionally in independent German rationalistic congregations, and perhaps among the Universalists, but not in a regular synod. A pious congregation well knows that by such a degradation of the holy office, which preaches reconciliation, and binds and looses in the name of Christ, it would degrade itself; and a minister, in any respectable church connection, would not be allowed to accept a call on such terms, even were he willing.

Favored by the general freedom of faith, all Christian denominations and sects, except the Oriental, have settled in the United States, on equal footing in the eye of the law; here attracting each other, there repelling; rivalling in both the good and the bad sense; and mutually contending through innumerable religious publications. They thus present a motley sampler of all church history, and the results it has thus far attained. A detailed description of these at present is forbidden, both by want of time and by the proportion of the discourse. Suffice it to say, in general, that the whole present distracted condition of the church in America, pleasing and promising as it may be, in one view, must yet be regarded on the whole as unsatisfactory, and as only a state of transition to something higher and better.

America seems destined to be the Phenix-grave not only of all European nationalities, as we have said above, but also of all European churches and sects, of Protestantism and Romanism. I cannot think that any one of the present confessions and sects, the Roman, or the Episcopal, or the Congregational, or the Presbyterian, or the Lutheran, or the German or Dutch Reformed, or the Methodist, or the Baptist communion, will ever become exclusively dominant there; but rather, that out of the mutual conflict of all something wholly new will gradually arise.

At all events, whatever may become of the American denominations and sects of the present day, the kingdom of Jesus Christ must at last triumph in the New World, as elsewhere, over all foes, old and new. Of this we have the pledge in the mass of individual Christianity in America; but above all, in the promise of the Lord, who is with his people always to the end of the world, and who has founded his church upon a rock, against which the gates of hell shall never prevail. And his words are yea and amen. . . .

America is the classic land of sects, where in perfect freedom from civil disqualification, they can develop themselves without restraint. This fact is connected indeed with the above-mentioned predominance of the Reformed type of religion. For in the Reformed church the Protestant features, and with them the subjective, individualizing principle, are most prominent. But in the term *sect-system* we refer at the same time to the whole ecclesiastical condition of the country. For there the distinction of church and sect properly disappears; at least the distinction of established church and dissenting bodies, as it is commonly understood in England and Germany. In America, there is, in fact, no national or established church; therefore no dissenter. There all religious associations, which do not outrage the general Christian sentiment and the public morality (as the Mormons, who, for their conduct, were driven from Ohio and Illinois), enjoy the same protection and the same rights. The distinction between confessions or denominations (as the word is there) and sects is therefore likewise entirely arbitrary, unless perhaps the acknowledgment or rejection of the ecumenical or old Catholic symbols be made the test; though this would not strictly apply even in Germany.

Favored by the general freedom of conscience, the representatives of all the forms of Christianity in the Old World, except the Greek—for we here leave out of view the isolated Russian colony in the Northwest of America—have gradually planted themselves in the vast field of the United States by emigration from all European countries, and are receiving reinforcements every year. There is the Roman with his Tridentinum and pompous mass; the Episcopal Anglican with his Thirty-nine Articles and Book of Common Prayer; the Scotch Presbyterian with his Westminster Confession, and his presbyteries and synods; the Congregationalist, or Puritan in the stricter sense, also with the Westminster Confession, but with his congregational independence; the Baptist, with his immersion and anti-paedobaptism; the Quaker, with his inward light; the Methodist, with his call to repentance and conversion, and his artificial machinery; the Lutheran, now with all his symbols, from the Augustana to the Form of Concord, now with the first only, and now with none of them; the German Reformed and Reformed Dutch, with the Heidelberg Cathechism and the Presbyterian Synodal church polity; the Unionist, either with the consensus of both confessions, or indifferently rejecting all symbols; the Moravian community, with its silent educational and missionary operations; and a multitude of smaller sects besides, mostly of European origin, but some of American. In short, all the English and Scotch churches and sects, and all branches of German and Netherland Protestantism, are there represented. Each one alone is, of course, weaker than its mother church in Europe, except the Puritanic, which has attained its chief historical importance only in New England. But they are all there, not rarely half a dozen in a single country town, each with its own church or chapel; and, where they have any real vitality at all, they grow there proportionally much faster than in Europe. Some, as the Presbyterian, the Methodist, the German Protestant, and the Roman Catholic, have even almost doubled their numbers within the last ten or twenty years.

This confusion of denominations and sects makes very different impressions on the observer from different theological and religious points of view. If he makes all of individual Christianity, and regards the conversion of men as the whole work of the church, he will readily receive a very favorable impression of the religious state of things in America. It is not to be denied that by the great number of churches and sects this work is promoted; since they multiply the agencies, spur each other on, vie with each other, striving to outdo one another in zeal and success. We might refer to the separation of Paul and Barnabas, by which one

stream of apostolic missionary labor was divided into two, and
fructified a greater number of fields with its living waters. There
are in America probably more awakened souls, and more individual effort and self-sacrifice for religious purposes, proportionally,
than in any other country in the world, Scotland alone perhaps
excepted. This is attributable, at least in part, to the unrestricted
freedom with which all Christian energies may there put themselves forth; and to the fact that no sect can rely on the favor
of the State, but that each is thrown upon its own resources, and
has therefore to apply all its energies to keep pace with its neigh-
bors and prevent itself from being swallowed up.

The charge that the sect system necessarily plays into the hands
of infidelity on one side and of Romanism on the other has
hitherto at least not proved true, though such a result is very
naturally suggested. There is in America far less open unbelief
and skepticism, than in Europe; and Romanism is extremely
unpopular. Whether things will continue so is a very different
question.

But on closer inspection the sect system is seen to have also its
weaknesses and its shady side. It brings all sorts of impure motives
into play, and encourages the use of unfair, or at least question-
able means for the promotion of its ends. It nourishes party spirit
and passion, envy, selfishness, and bigotry. It changes the peaceful
kingdom of God into a battle-field, where brother fights brother,
not, of course, with sword and bayonet, yet with loveless harsh-
ness and all manner of detraction, and too often subordinates the
interests of the church universal to those of his own party. It tears
to pieces the beautiful body of Jesus Christ, and continually
throws in among its members the firebrands of jealousy and dis-
cord, instead of making them work together harmoniously for
the same high and holy end. It should not be forgotten that
Christianity aims not merely to save individual souls, and then
leave them to themselves, but to unite them with God and therefore also with one another. It is essentially love, and tends towards
association; and the church is and ought to become more and
more the one body of Jesus Christ, the fullness of Him who filleth

all in all. If, therefore, the observer start with the conception of the church as an organic communion of saints, making unity and universality its indispensable marks, and duly weighing the many exhortations of Holy Scripture to keep the unity of the Spirit in the bond of peace; he cannot possibly be satisfied with the sect system, but must ever come out against it with the warnings of Paul against the divisions and parties in the Corinthian church. A friend very near to me, and a thoughtful, deeply earnest theologian, has keenly assailed and exposed the sect system as the proper American Antichrist. The noblest and most pious minds in America most deeply disapprove and deplore at least the sect *spirit*; and fortunately too, this spirit recedes in proportion as the genuine spirit of Christianity, the uniting and co-operative spirit of brotherly love and peace, makes itself felt. In the American Bible and Tract Societies and Sunday School Union, the various evangelical denominations work hand in hand and get along right well together, although their Catholicity is more of a negative character, not reconciling, but concealing the confessional differences, and although their charity is at an end as soon as the Romish church is mentioned, as if she was simply an enemy of Christ. Several of the most prominent churches maintain a friendly inter-delegation; and even in those which do not, or which make it a mere form, all the true children of God, when they see one another face to face, exchange the hand of fellowship in spite of all the jealousy and controversy between their respective communions.

Sectarianism, moreover—and this I might especially commend to the attention of German divines—is by no means a specifically American malady, as often represented; it is deeply seated in Protestantism itself, and is so far a matter of general Protestant interest. Suppose that in Prussia church and state should be suddenly severed; the same state of things would at once arise here. The parties now in conflict within the Established Church, would embody themselves in as many independent churches and sects, and you would have an Old Lutheran Church, a New Lutheran Church, a Reformed Church, a United Church—and that again divided into a union positively resting on the symbols, and a union acknowledging only the Scriptures—perhaps, also, a Schleiermacherian Church, and who knows how many spiritualistic and rationalistic sects and independent single congregations besides. America in fact draws all its life originally from Europe. It is not a land of *new* sects; for those which have originated there, as the Mormons, are the most insignificant, and have done nothing at all to determine the religious character of the people. It is only the rendezvous of all European churches and sects, which existed long before, either as establishments or as dissenting bodies. England and Scotland have almost as many different religious bodies as the United States, with the single difference that in the former countries one (the Episcopal in England, the Presbyterian in Scotland) enjoys the privilege of state patronage, while in America all stand on the same footing.

In forming our judgment of the American sect system, therefore, we are led back to the general question, whether Protestantism constitutionally involves a tendency towards denominationalism and sectarianism, wherever it is not hindered by the secular power. This we cannot so very easily deny. Protestantism is Christianity in the form of free subjectivity; of course not an unregenerate subjectivity, resting on natural reason—for this is the essence of rationalism—but a regenerate subjectivity, based on and submitting to the Word of God. It is thus distinguished from Catholicism, which takes Christianity in an entirely objective sense, as a new law, and as absolute authority, and does not therefore allow national and individual peculiarities at all their full right and free development. In the first, the centrifugal force predominates; in the second, the centripetal—there freedom, here authority. And to harmonize perfectly these two opposite yet correlative principles is the highest, but also the most difficult, problem of history.

Accordingly it is the great work and the divine mission of Protestantism to place each individual soul in immediate union with Christ and his Word; to complete in each one the work of redemption, to build in each one a temple of God, a spiritual church; and to unfold and sanctify all the energies of the individual. But, through the sinfulness of human nature, the principle of subjectivity and freedom may run out into selfish isolation, endless division, confusion, and licentiousness; just as the principle of objectivity, disproportionately applied, leads to stagnation and petrifaction; the principle of authority, to despotism in the rulers and slavery in the ruled. In North America, the most radically Protestant land, the constitutional infirmities of Protestantism, in religious and political life, are most fully developed, together with its energy and restless activity; just as the natural diseases of Catholicism appear most distinctly in the exclusively Roman countries of southern Europe.

Now in this unrestrained development and splitting up of Christian interests, most palpable in America, the Roman Catholic sees symptoms of an approaching dissolution of Protestantism and the negative preparation for its return into the bosom of the only saving church. But such a relapse to a position already transcended in church history, such an annulling of the whole history of the last three centuries, is, according to all historical analogy, impossible. How inconceivable that in this age of the general circulation of literature, the Book of all books can again be taken away from the people, and all the liberties, hard won by the Reformation, obliterated! Catholicism can, indeed, draw over to itself as it has lately done in Germany, England, and America, individuals, tired of the Protestant confusion and uncertainty, having no patience with the present, and no faith in the future, longing for a comfortable pillow of absolute, tangible authority. But Protestantism in the mass can never be swallowed up by it; or if it should be, it would soon break out again with increased violence, and shake the Roman structure still more deeply than it did in the sixteenth century.

We believe, indeed, by all means, that the present divided condition of Protestantism is only a temporary transition state, but that it will produce something far more grand and glorious than Catholicism ever presented in its best days. Protestantism after all still contains the most vigorous energies and the greatest activity of the church. It represents the progressive principle of history. It is Christianity in motion. Hence more may be expected from it than from the comparative stagnation of the Roman or Greek Catholicism. Converted regenerate individuals, these subjective Protestant heart-churches, are the living stones for the true Evangelical Catholic Church, which is to combine and perfect in itself all that is true and good and beautiful in the past. But this requires the previous fulfillment of the mission of Protestantism, the transforming of each individual man into a temple of God. Out of the most confused chaos God will bring the most beautiful order; out of the deepest discords, the noblest harmony; out of the most thoroughly developed Protestantism, the most harmonious and at the same time the freest Catholicism. What wild controversy has already raged, what violent passion has been kindled among theologians, about the doctrine of the Eucharist! And yet this sacrament is the feast of the holiest and deepest love, the symbol of the closest fellowship of Christ and the church. The one, holy, universal, apostolic church is an article not only of faith, but also of hope, to be fully accomplished only with the glorious return of Christ.

In America are found, in some degree, as a preparation for this great end, all the data for the problem of the most comprehensive union. For there, not only the Lutheran and Reformed confessions, but also the English and all the European sections and forms of the church are found in mutual attrition and in ferment. But, of course, Europe likewise, especially Germany and England, must have its part in the work; nay, must make the beginning. For Europe still stands at the head of Christian civilization, and is ever producing from her prolific womb new ideas and movements, which, through the growing facility, and frequency of intercommunication, the swelling emigration, and the exportation of elements of literature and culture of every kind, at once make themselves felt in America, perpetuate themselves there in modified forms, and come into immediate contact and conflict, so as to bury themselves in each other, and rise again as the powers of a new age in the history of the world and the church. Therefore have I called America, even in respect to religion and the church, the Phenix-grave of Europe.

NOTES

[1] As an aftermath of the 1848 revolution, a democratically elected constituent assembly met at Frankfurt (am Main) in 1848 and 1849. Its attempt to unify Germany under a federal constitution was not successful.

16

John Robert Godley

John Robert Godley (1814–1861) received a gentleman's education at Harrow and Christ Church, Oxford. Most of his life
was devoted to travel and government service. He was particularly interested in emigration and was partly responsible
for the establishment of a colony at Canterbury, New Zealand.
He came to America in 1844, but as a Tory and a high Anglican
he found little to admire. He had obviously been influenced by
the Oxford movement, which had been at its strongest during
his years at Christ Church, and saw in the weaknesses of the
voluntary system the fate which might be in store for England
if the Establishment was further weakened.

[*from* LETTERS FROM AMERICA]

T HE effect of the voluntary system upon the manner in which
the clergy perform their duties is not to be looked for chiefly
in a tendency to abstain from enforcing strictness of life, or
from preaching what are commonly called unwelcome truths
about sin and repentance, or even from rebuking individual
delinquents; as in all these things public opinion goes along with
and supports the minister: the more rigid his requirements, and
the more uncompromising his tone, the more will his flock
follow and applaud him. A man may therefore take what is
commonly called a high tone in matters of morality, with the
most complete impunity as regards his worldly interests, while

he may shrink from opposing the current of popular opinion where it is strongly and generally expressed: as, for instance, where plausible motives of expediency have induced irregular and self-chosen methods of pursuing what are admitted to be good ends. Of this nature are the "revivals," of which I have just spoken; and under the same category come all those unregulated societies with which New England is absolutely rife: abolition societies, advocating in many cases the grossly unscriptural principle that a slave may use force to obtain his freedom; non-resistance societies, which deny the lawfulness of assisting the civil and military executive against foreign or domestic enemies; and many others of a similar nature. Now I have reason to believe that few clergymen have, not merely opposed, but refused to join in advocating the objects of these societies with men whose conduct and expressions they cannot but condemn, where the feeling in favour of them has extensively pervaded their districts; while those who have opposed them have been obliged, in most cases, to resign. Again: I cannot conceive an American clergyman preaching the unlawfulness (on religious grounds) of the American Revolution (of course I am not speaking of any theory which might be considered subversive of the obligation to obey the government as at present constituted), and the duty of absolute submission to "the powers that be." I am not condemning the voluntary system; and indeed I may be wrong in supposing that men would shrink from expressing even such unpopular opinions as these if conscientiously convinced of their truth: I am only remarking that it is to such points as these that we ought to direct our attention in discussing the comparative advantages and evils of the system, and not, as is generally done, simply to the (so-called) moral tone of the preacher. There is no doubt thas, as far as such questions present a religious aspect (which they undoubtedly do), he ought not to hesitate to express his sentiments upon them: and the argument of those who disapprove of the voluntary system is that it tends to influence him unduly in this particular. . . .

I was much struck by a scene which I witnessed the other day while travelling in the interior. We stopped to change horses at a small tavern; the passengers collected round the fire in the bar-room, when the driver of the stage came in, and seeing a Bible lying on the chimney-piece, he opened it, and very deliberately read a chapter in a loud voice, every body remaining perfectly silent and attentive: when he had finished no comments were made, nor did any body appear to consider what he had done as at all out of place; it quite reminded one of the pilgrim fathers, their habits and their times.

Still, though such scenes may, perhaps, occasionally be even now met with in remote parts of the country, and though every where in New England the greatest possible decency and respect, with regard to morals and religion, is still observed, I have no hesitation in saying that I do not think the New-Englanders (or, indeed, the Americans generally, as far as I can judge) a *religious* people. The assertion, I know, is paradoxical, but it is nevertheless true; that is, if a strong and earnest *belief* be a necessary element in a religious character: to me it seems to be its very essence and foundation. I am not now speaking of belief in *the truth*, but belief in something or any thing which is removed from the action of the senses. Now I appeal to any candid American whether it be not the received doctrine among nine-tenths of his countrymen that creeds (religious dogmas, as they are called) are matters of no moment; that, so long as a man acts sincerely up to what he believes, he has as good a chance of salvation, *for he is as likely to be right*, as his neighbor; and that morality (so-called) is perfectly independent of, and infinitely more important than, religious belief. This is, I say, the avowed doctrine of the great majority now in America; and, as long as such is the case, outward morality may, indeed, prevail to a great extent (and I freely admit that in no country have I seen more appearances of it than in New England), under the influence of traditionary habits, enlightened self-interest, and the law of conscience; but there is no *religion*. No man can be said to believe in a religious system if he believes at the same time that another religious system has an equal chance of being true in the points

of difference which exist between them; for all religions profess
to be (as to their distinctive tenets) exclusively true, and propound doctrines to be believed as necessary to salvation: indeed,
it is impossible to conceive a religion that should not do so; such
a course would be not only shallow and unphilosophical, but
self-contradictory and suicidal. This is pre-eminently the case
with respect to Christianity; the apostolic epistles are filled with
passages which, had they been written by a modern theologian,
would have been branded as most intolerant and uncharitable:
there they stand, however, witnessing against the indifferentism
which I have described, proclaiming that if an angel from heaven
preach any other gospel he shall be accursed; and commanding us
not even to bid God speed to any that "bring not this doctrine."
But this is not all: scepticism, with respect to "peculiar religious
opinions," is quite inconsistent with a strong uncompromising
faith in what is super-sensual and eternal; the same mind which
rejects the evidence of the former cannot accept cordially, and
become fully convinced of, the latter. Men are generally unconscious of this themselves; their consciences tell them that they
ought to have a religion, and to act by its dictates: and they
think they do so, when they are, in fact, only acting as any
prudent, sensible, long-sighted person would act, if there were
no world beyond the grave, and no law revealed from heaven.
Self-denial, self-sacrifice, not temporary but permanent, to live
and to feel as a stranger and a pilgrim upon earth, and to look
upwards and forwards for a reward and a home—these constitute
the true tests of religious earnestness; and of these, though I
know there is little at home—comparatively little any where on
earth—I maintain that America presents even fewer symptoms
or appearances. I am not trusting to my own limited observation
in arriving at this conclusion: I find in M. de Tocqueville's work
an assertion of the same fact; he accounts for it, indeed, in a
different way, and attributes it (like every thing else, according
to his theory) to the operation of equality. I, on the contrary,
am inclined to think that the materialism thus admitted to exist
may chiefly be traced to the prevailing indifference with respect

to religious creeds; and that this indifference, again, is intimately connected with the compulsory neutrality of the government in religious matters. In public schools, in the halls of the legislature, in national institutions, all religions are placed upon an equality; chaplains are selected indiscriminately from each, as the majority of the day may happen to determine (one year, perhaps, a Roman Catholic, and the next a Unitarian); and the smallest preference of one religion to another, that is, the recognition of any definite, objective truth, would not be admitted for a moment. Now, this complete neutrality, entering, as it does, into so many parts of the system—every part, in fact, where men act in a corporate capacity—may be necessary; indeed, I feel it quite impossible, under the actual circumstances of the United States, even to suggest an alteration or a remedy: but surely the effect upon the public mind must be very prejudicial to earnestness and zeal; and without earnestness and zeal religion is a name—a lifeless form.

On the other hand, I am quite ready to admit that (as was, indeed, to be expected) there is little acrimony or bitterness entering into religious controversy in America: whether the absence of *odium theologicum* be attributable to indifference (as I think), or to charity (as an American would probably contend), the effect is undoubted, and, *pro tanto*, highly desirable. Few things constitute a subject for more self-gratulatory contrasts to Americans than the mutual hostility and the proselytizing spirit of European sects, compared with the "philosophical and comprehensive tone which is fashionable among religionists here." For my part, I prefer the earnest striving after truth, with its accompanying evil, to the carelessness about it, with its accompanying good. A party in Boston will comprise, generally, almost as many varieties of theological opinion as of individuals; and there will be no danger whatever of disagreeable discussions resulting therefrom: not merely is the subject tacitly suppressed, or set aside, as forbidden ground, but there is none of that embarrassment and awkwardness which it is hardly possible to avoid in the habitual intercourse of parties who, upon subjects which they have very much at heart, entertain radically opposite opinions, and which actually do appear, here as elsewhere, under *such* circumstances. A man who would feel himself embarrassed and uncomfortable if his next neighbour differed from him on the subject of a national bank, and who would certainly consider particular opinions about slavery as constituting a sufficient cause for avoiding the society of the man who held them, would express the most supreme and contemptuous indifference as to whether the rest of the party, with whom he was associating on the most intimate terms, were Christians or Mahometans, Heretics or Infidels. Is this habit reconcileable (I do not say in the case of every individual, but generally) with a true view of the relative importance of temporal and eternal interests? I have strong suspicions of the nature of that charity which leads to tolerance and "comprehensiveness" in religious matters alone, while upon all other subjects it leaves political rancour, party-feeling and personal hostility untouched by its influence.

Again: I never heard of a man taking a decidedly religious tone in Congress, that is openly professing Christian motives of action as influencing him in his legislative as well as his social capacity; indeed, I have reason to think that such a profession would expose him to jealousy and suspicion, as savouring of bigotry. I hope very many do act from such motives; but *that* public opinion cannot be in a healthy state which would forbid their being avowed. America ought to ask herself why she has no such statesmen to boast of as a Wilberforce, a Gladstone, and many others, who have not been ashamed to recognize publicly in the British House of Commons the existence of a law paramount to the code of political expediency, and to avow the duty of guiding their political career by its dictates. Where this is not the case— where either from indifference or fear of offence the members of the governing body in a state can consent to exclude, as inconvenient and out of place, all reference to those religious influences which ought to be continually present to their recol- lection, pervading and colouring every part of their moral being, there is imminent danger lest that state should sink to the level of a joint-stock company, combined for the mere purpose of securing the material interests of the partners, and political science, the επιστημη αρχιτεκτονικη [master design], be reduced there to the possesesion of a certain amount of economical knowledge and administrative dexterity.

I am perfectly aware that, in answer to these observations, an American will point to the churches and chapels of all denominations, which are to be found in very respectable numbers *in the better-peopled parts of the country*. I reply, that I am perfectly aware that a great majority of the people profess some religion—it is decent and proper so to do: an American, generally speaking, likes to see his wife and children go to meeting on Sundays (though he is not a great "church-goer" himself), and subscribes to his minister's salary as he does to the maintenance of the district school, or the village fire-engine, because he thinks him a useful instrument in promoting order and civilisation, and the "public good." What I complain of* is, not the absence of nominal, but of real, heart-felt, unearthly religion, such as led the puritan non-conformists to sacrifice country and kindred, and brave the dangers of the ocean and the wilderness, for the sake of what they believed to be God's truth. In my opinion, those men were prejudiced and mistaken, and committed great and grievous faults; but there was, at least, a redeeming element in their character—that of high conscientiousness: there was no compromise of truth, no sacrifice to expediency about them; they believed in the invisible, and they acted on that belief. Every where the tone of religious feeling, since that time, has been altered and relaxed; but, perhaps, nowhere so much as in the land where the descendants of those pilgrims live. . . .

It is difficult for an Englishman to realise the extreme laxity of American opinion upon these subjects, and the indifference with which the laity will adopt or depart from any given system of religious doctrines and ordinances. Numbers, especially among the more wealthy and educated classes, openly profess to belong

---

* These observations apply chiefly to the northern and central States. In the south and west I have good reason for thinking that there are very considerable numbers who *profess no religion*.

to no particular church, at the same time assuming to be "Christians," *i.e.* to believe in the inspiration of the Bible; while of those who hold the truth, a great part hold it accidentally, and, as it were, *heretically* (*i.e.* upon a principle of αγρεσιζ [sectarian adherence]), holding at the same time that they might just as lawfully and as safely have come to an opposite conclusion, and that a difference of opinion in religious matters no way differs in kind from a difference of opinion as to the comparative merits of Gothic or Grecian architecture, or German and Italian music. It is difficult to illustrate the prevailing tone on this subject by examples; but nobody can have associated or conversed much with Americans of all denominations without being very forcibly struck by it: it colours (often, as it were, unconsciously) the thoughts and language of the whole people. The American mind is essentially latitudinarian, and has a natural repugnance to any thing which affects an exclusive or dogmatical character. Like the ancient Romans, who would receive any number of *additional* divinities into their Pantheon, provided they did not interfere with those who were there already, the Americans will admit any sect to be Christian, Protestant, and orthodox (all which terms are generally considered as synonymous) which receives the Christian Scriptures, and any doctrinal scheme which it thinks may be deduced therefrom, so long as it allows all other to be equally right who do the same. Intellectually such "religionists" as these are far more formidable, because more consistent, than those who earnestly and believingly contend for an erroneous system; but, morally, their condition is infinitely less hopeful: and I look upon the preponderance of their sentiments as a very unfavourable prognostic for the progress of Catholic views in America.

Again: the tone and spirit of *democracy* is essentially opposed to Catholic views. I do not for a moment mean to assert that it is irreconcileable with them (still less do I, as a Catholic, maintain that any one form of government is of immutable obligation as peculiarly conformable to the Divine will); I know that a person may draw a clear, logical distinction between theological and political matters, as lying in distinct, incommensurable provinces; and that, while in the former he is humble, child-like, submissive to authority, patient of mystery, more ready to believe than to argue, and continually looking out of himself for assistance and support, in the latter, he may be independent, self-relying, a sturdy stickler for his rights, and a contemner of the powers that be, unless they prove to his entire satisfaction that they ought to be. I know that these diversities of mental action coexist in some men, and that many more imagine that they coexist in themselves; but nothing will convince me that *in general* it will be so, or that *a nation* will ever be characterised at the same time by strong practical republicanism and a faithful reception of the Catholic system of theology.* The reception by a people of any religious system will (humanly speaking) depend chiefly upon the prevalent habits of thought and feeling which exist among them; for our reason is biassed by our affections, and our religious views are developed far more by means of a moral than an intellectual process. The religious system, when established, will itself react, no doubt, and modify to a very important extent the national character; but where it has to make its own way, its chances of success, according to our limited perception of the relation of causes and effects, depend, not only upon the truth and beauty of its doctrines, but upon the temper of mind which, as it were, meets them: and, therefore, I do not see much prospect at present of any great or permanent progress being made by the church among the mass of the American people. Independently of metaphysics, indeed, there are great obstacles in her way, from that jealousy which has always been

* American churchmen are fond of saying that their theological opinions make no difference in their politics. They must excuse me for doubting the fact. I know that among a pretty extensive acquaintance I never met but one who had adopted decided high-church views, and who retained the slightest tendency towards ultra-democracy in politics. I admit that a man may be perfectly sincere and strictly logical in holding both; but so it is, that they do not. Indeed, I have generally observed that churchmen of the Anglo-American communion take but little part or interest, generally speaking, in politics. They seem to feel instinctively that, under existing circumstances they would not be in their element if they did.

felt towards her, as well on account of her Anglican propensities, and the recently-revived ecclesiastical intercourse between the mother and the daughter church, as also on account of the alleged aristocratic character and pretensions of her members. . . .

It is impossible to imagine a more painful contrast than this, which must strike every churchman, between the manner in which ecclesiastical affairs are managed in America and in England; and I have no hesitation in expressing my conviction that if the disadvantages and incapacities under which the Church of England now labours be the necessary result of her connection with the state, the latter ought to be relinquished, rather than the former permanently submitted to. I feel deeply the advantages of that connection; I should be grieved indeed that the state should cease to recognize the existence of religious truth, by professing and supporting the Apostolic Faith; I should dread the judgments which might well be expected to follow upon its doing so: but I can never forget that we have prior obligations and higher duties than those of citizens and subjects, and that we are therefore by no means concluded by an appeal to our sense of the latter; a writ of error lies to a superior court. I cannot, however, see that there is any incompatibility between freedom of ecclesiastical action in all things necessary or desirable, and a far more intimate connection than that which exists in England between the church and the temporal power. Difficulties may no doubt arise, and occasionally confusion of jurisdictions, from the mixed nature of the subject matter, but there is no reason to suppose that they would be insuperable: and, even if they were greater than they are, it would be necessary to grapple with them; for it is plainly impossible that the present state of things, giving to one party all its own way, and forbidding another to open its mouth, can be permanently maintained. It is defective alike in theory and in practice.

17

James Dixon

James Dixon (d. 1871) was an English Methodist clergyman. He entered the ministry in 1812 and in 1841 was chosen to be president of the annual British Wesleyan Conference. In 1848 he was sent to represent British Methodism at the quadrennial General Conference of American Methodism at Pittsburgh. There he performed the salutary function of reminding the Methodist delegates that though the northern and southern branches had separated in 1844, northern Methodism still had not dealt adequately with the moral implications of slavery. Dixon combined his official duties with a tour of the United States and Canada. His book, published the following year, was primarily intended, as Dixon put it, "to make the Methodist body in England acquainted with the state and progress of their system of religion in the United States."[1] He did find opportunity however, to make some more general observations, including the following on the circumstances of the Christian faith in America.

[*from* METHODISM IN AMERICA]

IT is, then, an undoubted fact, that the American people do pay great regard to religion; and as this, like every thing else, is with them a personal and not a conventional concern, it is all the more energetically promoted. It seems a principle of Americanism that the obligations of our nature are untransferable. An American never dreams of putting his social or religious obligations into commission. He never considers himself as having denuded himself of his responsibilities when he has given his vote for a president, and taken his share in constructing a government. Even his political duties are not, in his own estimation, put in abeyance by these transactions, much less his moral and religious. He does not expect the government to serve God for him, or to take into its hands the task of publicly providing for that conservation of morality and religion which he knows can only be secured by personal exertions.

According to American ideas, the state does not consist of public functionaries, whether civil or ecclesiastical, but of the people. The souls and bodies of the population, unitedly, constitute the state: not a function, not an office. In the state making provision for this or the other, the American would include himself. He has no notion of public men taking his place, and relieving him of the burden of his own intelligence, conscience, humanity. . . .

How, then, seeing that every American is expected to act for himself, is he prepared to take his post? Let us examine this point. Its solution is what we want to get at. Is he let loose on the world a mere animal to prey upon its vitals, or is he religiously prepared? This leads us to the question of education. Great attention is paid by the Americans to this vital subject. What would be called in this country national education, universally prevails. Schools are provided at the public expense; and though this people have a proverbial antipathy to taxation, yet they willingly tax themselves for this purpose. The system so often attempted here, on the model of some of the continental nations, is not the system of America. They have not established a central power, or educational department, under a minister of state, or any thing analogous to our Committee of Privy Council. The people manage their own affairs in this as in other things. The municipal bodies and the parochial authorities have the power to assess themselves for educational purposes. This is done on a broad scale; in the elder States the provision is universal, so that every child may, if his parents choose, obtain the advantages of a good common education. And inasmuch as every inhabitant is obliged to pay his share of the expense, whether he avails himself of the school or not, this is found to operate against parental neglect. But the advantages are so obvious; the popular voice against ignorance, and in favour of knowledge, is so influential; the duties of citizenship, in which all share, are so pressing, and its honours so tempting; that every parent is induced to place his children in one of these schools.

Zealous partisans would probably say that these are not religious schools, because particular creeds are not enforced. This would be impossible in a country where no creed possesses a pre-eminence, or is sanctioned by the state. But if the holy scriptures constitute the basis of Christianity, then these are Christian schools, notwithstanding the absence of creeds. The Bible is read daily, it is the standard book, the foundation of every thing; and its divine authority is thus universally taught, and its sacred lessons constantly inculcated. True to their principles, the Romanists at New-York, some time ago, attempted to get the Bible banished from the public schools. In this they failed; for though by their union and compactness they possess much strength, and on merely political questions, by throwing their weight into one scale, they have it in their power to turn the balance, on this point, which was deemed a religious one, and on which all the Protestants were agreed, they utterly failed in their unholy attempt.[2]

This educational provision, being purely popular, may be taken as an indication of the public mind on a great religious question. Instead of leaving their children to go astray from their birth, we see that Christian instruction is provided for them, as an essential and national blessing. This does not seem as if the people were indifferent to Christianity; and, moreover, it proves that they desire to seize the most fitting time in the life of man to inculcate its sacred lessons. This, no doubt, is one of the healing ingredients thrown into the troubled waters, one of the moral forces which ever after works in determining the character of the individual, the state of domestic life, and the conditions of society. And instead of indifference in this one arrangement, we see religion, in its most catholic form, employed as an instrument of national order, virtue, and peace; and, that a useful and virtuous citizenship is not expected without the employment of suitable means.

We are considering the question of religion. Do the Americans trust to the processes of secular knowledge, or the power of merely human means, for the maintenance of public order, and social prosperity? The answer to this question stands out in bold relief. In every city, small and great, are seen large and spacious public buildings; and, on inquiry, the stranger is told that these are the common day-schools of the place. On entering he finds that, besides the routine of a very good educational system, embracing the usual matters of secular instruction, the scriptures are taught to the whole population; God speaking to them in the impressive lessons of his own word. Here the work of Christianity begins. Can any one calculate the amount of influence produced on the public mind, and on the moral state of a great people, by this one living, active, pervading agency? Religion is here brought to operate upon the youthful heart in its blandest and most winning, attractive form; namely, that of the words of scripture. It is not so very evident as some persons seem to imagine, that the best way to impress the mind of children is to drill them to get by heart some metaphysical, crabbed dogmas of theology which neither themselves nor their teachers can in the least degree comprehend. Yet, in the jargon of our sectarianism, this is called teaching religion, whilst the reading of the Bible itself is considered as not teaching religion at all; and schools *only* using the word of God, with prayer, are said to be secular. Certainly, Americans do not think so. The holy scriptures are a reality with them; and by their conduct, we have reason to think that they place more confidence in the divine teaching of these "lively oracles" of God than they do in the step-by-step process of Catechisms, all of which begin at the wrong end; commence at the top and build downwards; start with the highest abstractions on the divine essence and attributes, and then from this elevation lead the poor little inquirer down into the details and facts of revelation. Is not a population formed on the inculcation of the scripture as likely to become real Christians and good citizens as a population drilled in the abstractions of any existing Catechism? There is a breadth, a fulness, a simplicity, and especially a divinity, in the word of God, which cannot be found any where else; and, least of all, in the *bare-bone*, skeleton-like lessons propounded to the poor children of this nation. On the whole, then, it must be seen that the entire American people are trained in religion from their childhood, if the Bible teaches it. At any rate, an impression is made as to the divine authority of this holy book, that it is the word of God, the charter of salvation, the guide to heaven, and the only rule of faith and practice binding on the human conscience. One would think this is doing something towards forming society, and building the morals, happiness, and progress of the nation on our glorious Christianity.

But besides the care taken of the young, we find that Christianity pervades the United States in vigorous action. This is seen in the numbers attending public worship, in the extent of church-communion, in the observance of the sacraments of the church, in the respect paid to the sabbath, in the number and variety of religious and charitable institutions, in the placing of their collegiate and higher educational departments under the care generally of religious men, in the diffusion and influence of a Christian literature; and, in fine, by the depth and extent of religious feeling and principle. By these means, Christianity, it is evident, touches and influences the entire social and political state.

It is not meant by this that every individual is a pious Christian, but that the spirit of the evangelical system is in sufficient power to give to religious opinion and sentiment the complete ascendant in society. A man is not reflected upon, or deemed less fit for the higher duties of the state, by belonging to a Christian church; he is rather considered the better qualified for even civil posts of trust and responsibility. It happened that the writer fell in with persons, and heard from them the declaration that they could not give their suffrages to a very favourite candidate for the presidential chair, on the ground that he was thought to be too lax in his habits. And, moreover, it was said again and again, that this gentleman had damaged his position and blighted his prospects by this very circumstance. Afterwards, indeed, he had reformed; and it was stated, on good authority, that this gentleman had joined a Christian church, so that this objection must have fallen to the ground. This will appear foolish and bigoted to many of the wise men of this world, and may be thought to have been the feeling only of hot-headed enthusiasts. Not so. And it illustrates the point for which it is adduced, namely, that Christianity is a very powerful element in American society.

A very sensible and amiable gentleman, living in the States, remarked, on the voyage out, "One of the things which will surprise you is the number of sects existing in the country." By the by, there is not much difference in this respect between the mother and the daughter. But the fact here stated is a great stumbling-block to many, who can entertain no idea favourable to religion itself unless it exist as a unity, and is placed under the leadership of their favourite ecclesiastical functionaries. Certainly such parties will not find their "ideal church" in America. But if they will look deep enough, they will discover what is better than an external organization of stupidity and death; they will find very much of the vitality of Christianity, a settled and active faith, together with a profound conviction of the obligations to energetic piety, and the exercise of a divine charity.

This division of the Christian body in America into sects, and the fact that a union with any one of these sects is no bar against employments of the most honourable kind, is, to us, an anomaly. A Methodist lord-chancellor, a Baptist attorney-general, a Presbyterian commander of the forces, an Independent secretary of the state, and an Episcopal, or Popish, gentleman doomed to take rank with one of these sectarians, or under him, as the case may be, looks strange in this country. This is no fictitious picture, but a matter of fact. Men are united in the common service of their country indiscriminately, irrespective of their creed or religious connexions. The sects may hate each other, as is their wont elsewhere; but the state knows no distinction betwixt one class of religionists and another.

At the present moment, though I was told that the President does not hold communion with any church; yet he usually listens to a Methodist sermon in the morning, from one of the chaplains of Congress, who is of that persuasion, and to a Presbyterian minister in the evening, his lady belonging to that church. One of the judges of the Supreme Court, answering as nearly as possible to our Court of Chancery, is at this moment a member of the Methodist Episcopal body, not nominally, but really; observing the rules, and attending upon all the services, of his church in all his movements. Moreover, the talents, character, and standing of this gentleman are such that in the present contest for the office of president he has been mentioned, indeed brought forward by a numerous and most respectable class of his fellow-citizens, as a candidate for the high distinction. These are only mentioned as instances of the working of the system; and no doubt every other appointment is in agreement with these cases of perfect impartiality.

But the matter of fact is that in the United States the several churches to which reference is made are not, in our sense of the expression, sects at all. There are no sects in America, no Dissenters, no seceders—or, whatever other term may be employed to designate the position and standing of a Christian society. They are all alike considered as Christians; and adopting, according to the judgment of charity, with equal honesty the common charter of salvation, the word of God, they are treated as equal, and as possessing similar and indefeasible rights.

This is certainly a new aspect of living and visible Christianity; and our business with it at present is, to test its operations on society. Can perfect liberty and equality in religion work well when favoured by circumstances as in the United States? Is Christianity itself, in its own revelations, its own glorious platform and basis, its own provisions and divinity, when made plain, and put into the hands of a people, sufficient, without being formed and modified by the political society, to produce its

legitimate fruits? This question, like many others, is in course
of solution in the States. Go into a popish country, and speak of
Christianity, and the native of one of these nations, however
elevated in rank, or polished by education, instantly thinks of
Popery. He knows of no religious system but the hierarchy
of Rome; and it is impossible to get into his head an idea of an
abstract, a divine, and an unalterable Christianity, reposing on the
truth of God, and connected with his throne. It is very much the
same amongst ourselves, and especially amongst the higher ranks.
These gentlemen cannot conceive of any Christianity otherwise
than that which is embodied in their own church. In almost all
the speculations of men amongst us, church organizations, official
distinctions, ecclesiastical canons, and the dress and tinsel which
men put upon their own fond creations, are confounded with
Christianity itself, and so called. If looked at only in this light,
the evangelical economy must be pronounced an utter failure.
Of all the wretched things whose history stands out in the annals
of time, the history of churches is the most humiliating, and the
most calculated to make human nature blush. What has ecclesiastical, hierarchical Christianity done for the world in ancient
times? It has put its trammels upon the simple, primitive, and
personal piety and usefulness, which had been produced from
time to time by the pure gospel, and reduced the so-called church
to the condition of one mighty conglomerated mass of stupid
ignorance and vice; then, seizing the reins of even political power,
has entwined itself parasitically around the institutions of society,
reducing the world to the dominion of a politico-religious
despotism.

Much debate has arisen in the world respecting states adopting
the church, then corrupting, then enslaving, her. In passing, it
may be permitted one to ask the zealous partisans of church
purity and state corruption, of church love of freedom and state
love of tyranny, just to reverse their inquiries, and ask, in all
possible candour, as to the real delinquents in this matter. My
belief is that, as a general rule, the state has not corrupted the
church, except as a participant, just as companions in vice vitiate

each other; but the church has, in most instances, corrupted the state. Neither has the state enslaved the church, as a general rule, though sometimes this may have been the case; but the church has, whenever it was allowed, invariably enslaved the state. Nothing is so detrimental to the liberties and the virtues of mankind as a corrupt, a fetid religion, at the same time organized and guided by the subtle and crafty genius of a profligate priesthood.

It can be no matter of surprise that the American people, being favoured with the opportunity, the soil being clear, and no old institutions standing in the way, should be disposed to adopt a new principle, and, discarding all authoritative church-organization, try the effect of Christianity, itself, in its own native grandeur and divine simplicity. This they have done. We have seen that the people is the state; and the state, in this sense, namely, through the people, has, with the exception of the infidels amongst them, adopted Christianity; only, instead of being an hierarchical government, it is that of the holy Scriptures—the Bible itself being the governing light, the decisive authority, the court of final appeal. All the interests of society converge to this point; religion is its life, its power, its beauty. It is like the *substrata* of the world, on which all the soils whence the vegetable productions spring repose in security.

Is this common Christianity, taught and developed in Scripture, sufficient for a nation? May the people of a state be safely left, other things being favourable, to this simple process? The answer to this question is in course of solution in the United States. So far as it has been tested, it is believed to have answered. Nothwithstanding the number of churches, bearing different names, and adopting diversified forms of service, there is probably as much or more unity in these States than elsewhere. Looking at their spirit and visible position; that is, in the general absence of polemic strife, of bitter contentions between church and church, of acrimonious declamation against each other in their religious periodicals; and then their intercommunion and good neighbourhood, joint exertions for common objects, and, on the whole, harmonious agreement—these all unite to show that these professors of the name of Christ can meet each other on the ground of their common Christianity, though differing in non-essential points. So far as he had the opportunity of intercourse with ministers and Christians of various denominations, the author is bound to say that he met with the most frank and affectionate courtesy, and saw the same spirit manifested one to another; and, moreover, that there appeared infinitely less of what is distinctive and sectarian than in this country. Whilst at the Conference at Pittsburgh, all the Protestant pulpits of every sort were filled each Sunday by Methodist ministers, except some one or two of the Episcopal churches, whose ministers were believed to be tinctured with Puseyism.

It is no marvel that this unity of spirit prevails. The bitterness of sectarianism is prevented by the nature of their position. No one church thinks of calling another church, resting on the Scriptures as its basis, and only differing in external organization, "heretics," "schismatics," and "Dissenters." No class of ministers, except popish priests and a few hair-brained Puseyites, ever dream of saying of other ministers that they are "unauthorized," have no "vocation," are "intruders" into other men's folds, and "usurpers" of the priestly office. These things can have no existence where common-law Christianity prevails; they are the assumptions of sects, of exclusive pretensions, of caste claims. The only unity that ever can be found in this world—unless God miraculously cut down all souls to one common level—is this. No power on earth can screw mankind into one shape and form on matters of faith and religious opinion. Unity can never exist in the sense of sameness, like bricks in a wall, or metal from a die. What is to throw souls into the same type? The idea is absurd; but this kind of unity has ever been the cant of bigots, or oftener still the instrument of tyrants to obtain the object of their ambition— dominion over their fellow-men. The unity of the gospel lies deeper; it is unity in the truth, not as seen by another, but as apprehended by the individual mind. But this truth is large, broad, open. The divine revelations are not given in set and limited propositions, like the syllogisms of man. It seems to be the purpose of God to leave the *manner* of apprehending and believing the gospel undefined and free. How should it be otherwise? Give any dogma to the first dozen men who may be met with, and it is certain that every one will conceive of it differently. How, then, can unity be found in the *manner* of holding the truth? But though the gospel may be apprehended variously, yet, if it is really embraced, and simply believed, as the mind is assisted by the helps within its reach, and especially as taught by the Spirit, who shall say that this vitiates the truth itself?

Hence, though in the United States the churches may be called by different names, and there may be diversities of opinion, even in matters of faith; yet it does not follow from this that they are not every one of them true churches. But it is more on points of discipline and church order, than on questions of truth and faith, that differences spring up, and become the prolific parents of separations. Can any one prove from holy scripture, that the Author of Christianity has not left this an open question? Or, can any one show that He has given his followers a model church, a platform, a skeleton temple? He has done no such thing. In his mercy and goodness to mankind, He has—following the analogies of nature—prepared a world, a universe of truth and grace, appearing confused, but not so in reality, stretching infinitely beyond the line and definitions of man. And just as men are left to build their social state and polity, in the midst of the agencies and provisions of nature; to cultivate their fields, erect their cities, appropriate to themselves the bounties of Providence, and create the forms of civilization for themselves; so, in like manner, Christians are permitted to erect their tents, found their churches, and enjoy the blessings of religion freely, on the broad field of scriptural truth; and, for any thing which can be shown to the contrary, one organization is as lawful as another; the only difference being in the fitness of such organization to edify the people themselves, and evangelize the world without.

The American system looks for unity on this broad basis. As far as can be seen, it is as much secured as can be well expected in the midst of the infirmities of human nature. At any rate, society is not convulsed, nor the state put into jeopardy, by religious contentions, claims, and projects. If religion does not bless, neither does it curse, the country; if it does not produce health, neither does it extend any social pestilence; if, in fine, it does not allay human passions, neither does it exasperate them. But the matter is placed too low by being thus hypothetically put. It is my deep conviction that religion is the conservative power of American society. It is the salt of the community: it is the life and the soul of public and private virtue: it is the cement, the power of coherence, which holds the States together; and, by purifying the public morals, elevating the soul with noble sentiments, creating the sense of responsibility, and stimulating to industry, it is creative of their greatness and power.

NOTES

[1] James Dixon, *Methodism in America* (London: for the author, 1849), p. iii.

[2] This controversy, which contributed to the felt need of American Catholics for a parochial school system, is discussed in Stokes, Vol. I, pp. 827–32.

18

Camille Ferri-Pisani

In the summer of 1861 Prince Napoleon, cousin of the French
Emperor Napoleon III and nephew of Napoleon Bonaparte,
arrived in New York for a visit to the United States. His party
included a French officer of Corsican ancestry, Lieutenant
Colonel Camille Ferri-Pisani, who served as his aide-de-camp.
Ferri-Pisani's letters describing the visit were published in 1862
as *Lettres sur les Etats-Unis d'Amérique*. There is little that is
remarkable in most of his account. At best it consists of candid
observations on that early phase of the Civil War when the
outcome was very much in doubt. In the final letter, however,
Ferri-Pisani reveals his interest in the voluntary system of religious organization as one of the most intriguing aspects of
American life. Most provocative are his reflections on the
place of Catholicism in this system and on the relative capacity
of Catholicism and Protestantism to meet the challenge of
rationalism.

[*from* PRINCE NAPOLEON IN AMERICA]

TODAY the United States presents very moving and disturbing
spectacles. Armies are fighting on all points of her huge territory.
The race which, it was thought, would realize the peaceful ideal
of modern mankind is suddenly changed into a warlike nation
torn from within. A frightened Europe wonders if the New
World is not entering the heroic age, if the New World is not
destined to go through all the fatal phases marking the historical
development of the oldest nations. On the other hand, slavery—

whether it be the cause or pretext of these horrifying conflicts—stands amidst the horrors of war as a question of life and death, in front of which philosopher, statesman, and economist alike recoil. Well, all these extraordinary facts which we are witnessing and which someday will fill the pages of this century's history have, in my eyes, a less formidable bearing than what we have just seen in Boston. This city is the stage of one of these significant happenings which transform man's condition without, however, leaving marks of blood and fire in his memory—like the great political events. I mean the establishment of deism in the New World as a religion, a church. No longer is it deism taught by a speculative philosophy, but rather deism practiced as a cult and a moral and social principle by the American elite and making terrifying progress to the detriment of Protestantism. . . .

In the beginning the constitutional provision of the colony granting citizenship only to the members of a congregation was applied exclusively to the *saints*. It was a pure theocracy. In its rigorism, the system became impracticable. Under a democratic regime, four fifths of the male and adult population of the colony could not be excluded from any participation in the public affairs and treated as pariahs because they had not received grace. Even in the seventeenth century this was too much! The *saints* made a concession. They granted political rights to those who renewed solemnly the vow of baptism and who were given a certificate of morality and religious faith by an assembly of the *saints*. Thus a certain number of colonists entered the state though remaining at the door of the church.

No doubt you want to know how the *saints* were recruited in each congregation?

Today the candidates are admitted by the assembly of the *saints* after a public profession of faith and a check on their moral behavior and religious life—tested over a long period of time. I suspect that this criterion, flexible, vague, and more moral than mystic, was a concession to the modern mind. In the seventeenth century, the entrance examination was, I believe, much more dogmatic, more special, and nearly freed of any element except that of grace. The question was to find out whether or not the sinner had been regenerated, renewed through an insufflation of the divine spirit at a given day and time. It was a psychological analysis rather than religious and moral. No doubt the questions and answers must have varied infinitely according to the prevailing conception of the dogma in the given congregation. At any rate, we can be sure that with the help of fanaticism and mysticism, these inquiries into an individual's conscience must have revealed, more than once, very singular doctrines on the method used by the Divinity to communicate with man. Undoubtedly they often understood it in a nearly material sense, and there must have been cases when the *saints* questioned a candidate about his so-called regeneration just as a doctor questions a patient on the moment he felt the first feverish shiver. Such was the system of the colony for about 150 years.

It was difficult for the modern spirit to penetrate this Middle Ages fortress. Shortly before the War of Independence, the Massachusetts legislature was forced to admit and tolerate the Episcopal Church. Not only were the members of this church given the right to worship, but also they were exempted from the parish tax feeding the treasury of the state church. In 1780, as most of the states reformed their constitutions, the liberal movement which swept the nation carried along the old Massachusetts Puritans. Virginia adopted Jefferson's famous declaration of religious tolerance, which in his mind was more a manifesto of atheism than a homage to freedom. The other states imitated Virginia, some exceeding it, others remaining behind, according to the strength and popularity of the bonds formerly tying them to a state church. Some declared that henceforth civil society would no longer be concerned with religious matters. Others recognized all Christian churches; while others only the Protestant sects, that is they granted political rights only to members of these churches. In several states they still maintained the religious tax, but they reorganized it on the principle of a proportional distribution among the various churches.

In Massachusetts the legislature granted the status of citizenship to all Christians independently of their sects or communions. Furthermore, the legislature decreed that the individual religious tax would be paid to the sect chosen by the individual. You might believe that this took away from the Congregational Church its character and privileges of state church; it was not completely so! What they kept of it for another fifty years was sufficient to have the most disastrous effect on the religious spirit. The religious circumscriptions were maintained, and only those persons belonging authentically and effectively to another Christian religion were exempted from the religious tax. Thus, each Congregational Church was enriched by the contributions of the large crowd of persons indifferent to religious matters. The result was very remarkable: a large number of persons, completely unconcerned with religion, opposed paying their money to a church they did not frequent while living under a system of liberty. They tried hard to circumvent the law by the foundation of dissident cults, with a rather suspect orthodoxy, but whose existence sufficed to take away some of the funds usually going to the Congregationalists. Several sects—Christian in name only, and which eventually increased considerably—owe their origin to this singular obstinacy of legislators who insisted upon maintaining a national church.

Meanwhile, the principle of the separation of church and state prevailed successively in all the states of the Union, with Massachusetts lagging far behind. The new idea—put into practice in all parts of the country with the customary ardor of the Americans for a material or moral discovery—assaulted the old Puritan principle from all sides. In 1820 the Massachusetts legislature thought it was making an important concession: they abolished all legal distinction between the *saints* and the others. Like all concessions extorted from people who hesitate between two opposed principles without being able to make up their minds, this one was disastrous for everybody. The religious spirit lost the support of a restricted class which was completely under the spell of tradition and which had resisted the various encroachments of the generally rationalistic heresies. The crowd of parishioners, skeptical, envious, and avid for scandal, when suddenly asked to choose the pastor and to decide about spiritual matters alongside the *saints*, introduced all kinds of novelties which dealt a deadly blow to the Congregational Churches. Several congregations were invaded by doctrines completely hostile to Congregationalism and even opposed to the Christian idea. Several ancient families, who were proud of tracing their ancestry back to the Pilgrims or to the Puritans of Winthrop, abandoned the temple where both their fathers and themselves had worshiped God in the same way and looked for other asylums far from the sanctuaries soiled by scandalous heresies. This period of transition was very painful for religion. No one could trust his brother, his pastor, or even his own faith. Finally, in 1831, the legislators decided to resort to the only remedy which might prevent a complete religious dissolution; they decreed, more than thirty years after the other states, the separation of churches, whatever they might be, from the state.

As soon as the last trace of the ancient Puritanism was erased from the constitution of Massachusetts, the Congregational churches of this state began their work of free and voluntary recomposition similar to that which had restored the Episcopal Church in the Southern states at the beginning of the century. Each parish was reorganized on a personal basis, no longer according to territorial divisions. Under the law the congregations were only civil societies, owning buildings, with particular contracts with certain persons—their pastors.

The history of the Congregational churches can be chosen to illustrate the general development of Protestantism in America. However, the phase it has reached today—a voluntary system—if isolated from the teachings furnished by the other sects, could produce some confusion in the mind. It so happened, through circumstances independent of each other, that as the voluntary system gave new vigor to the social and, in a way, religious existence of the Congregational churches, their spiritual existence was poisoned by the doctrines of rationalism and deism. It would be unjust to blame the voluntary system—which is of a temporal and human order—for purely religious phenomena, because the latter only take place in the conscience and belong exclusively to the domain of ideas. The voluntary system contributed to Congregationalism all the good that a good social constitution can give to a religion. One cannot ask an organization which handles only the temporal interests of a church to account for its spiritual interests. When the religious faith changes or fades away, when the souls vacillate and bow under the breath of a modern philosophy, when the dogma disappears in vapor through too much epuration, one must look for the causes of these transformations elsewhere rather than in the ephemeral regulations invented by legislators for the use of religious and civil societies. One must look for them in the natural laws which preside over the intellectual development of mankind.

Thus, to judge the voluntary system, one must examine the situation in which all of the religions and sects in the United States were placed by its influence. I certainly would not want to express, not even to have, an opinion on the following question: should we maintain some bond between civil and religious society or is it better completely to separate the church from the state? It is a question of an unmeasurable gravity, still I might mention the following fact: America is the only country in the world where they have put the voluntary system into practice (complete separation of church and state) and there was not a single voice that did not proclaim the excellence of this system.

Naturally, I only count the opinions of the truly religious men, those who subordinate temporal interests to those of Heaven— there are many such men in America, ministers, priests, pastors, and particularly the Catholic clergy. It is to be expected that the enemies of religion—as Jefferson was—or simply the indifferent, always were and remain in favor of the systematic abstention of the law in religious matters. Their voices bear no meaning as to the value of the system. It is quite different with the unanimous and sincere support given to the *voluntary* system today by all the scrupulous and fervent consciences who had accepted it in the past as a fateful necessity. Enlightened by experience, there is not one of them who regrets losing the protection of the state and its tutelary and disguised intervention in religious matters.

It is doubtful whether the political power—even if it had assembled all the creative faculties of the country—could have done for religion what the *voluntary* system has done in the last fifty years in the United States. One must not forget that in 1800—and for many causes which I cannot reveal to you— religion in America, no matter the sect, presented the saddest spectacle from the temporal point of view as well as from the spiritual. I just described the confusion of the Congregational Church around 1820. In Virginia the Episcopal Church had lost sixty-three churches (out of ninety-one) in 1800, and did not have a single episcopate. At the same epoch, there were only twenty-six Catholic priests and not a single bishopric.

The increase and achievement of the Christian churches in the last fifty years is unmeasurable, and out of proportion to the real increase in population. To give you an idea of the impulse which the *voluntary* system gave to religion, I will just mention that more than 1,000 new churches are built each year in this country; as many new ministers, pastors, or priests are consecrated. If there were in the United States a Ministry of Religion (as in France), the yearly increase in the budget of this department would be from twelve to fifteen million, much more than one third of the average amount of our budget for religion.

The Catholic religion is the one which has made the most progress. I am not talking of conversions from one religion to another; I am not interested in the detailed account of the lost and gained souls. This point of view, the most interesting for both Catholic and Protestant churches, has resulted in many contra- dictory assertions. It is practically impossible to know whether there are more Catholics converting to Protestantism or vice versa. Whatever the source of the increase of the Catholic element in America (natural increase of the population, Irish emigration, conversions), it is undeniable that this increase is considerable. The Catholic clergy follows, even precedes this movement; it has increased its means of action as rapidly as the religious needs of the population. They have the nicest churches in the United States; their seminaries attract attention because of their splendid developments and the luxury of their construction. The Catholic priests are cited as models of virtue, piety, and charity. The bishops have great influence and enjoy great consideration. Their financial resources are considerable; some are gifts to the church for charity, instruction, and the cult; others are just deposited in the hands of the clergy by their parishioners. The Irish, for example, feel safe only when they entrust their savings to the bishop. The Archbishop of New York is much more important than any of our archbishops. He meets the President on an equal basis and gives or withdraws his support—not as an archbishop, but as an influential citizen. If the bishops do not enjoy the prestige attached to the administrative hierarchy, they console themselves with the thought that they are not absorbed by it and that they have better things to do than to worry about matters of precedence. They are not represented in the Senate; they do not appear on the Budget. On the other hand, they do not receive ministerial instruction or censure, and the list of voluntary contributions is far more productive than their salary could ever be. As they are not master in other people's houses, they are masters at home, that is to say, in their schools, seminaries, convents, and churches. Finally, if they never ask for or receive privileges, they often appeal to the common right. When they think they were wronged in their rights—which are none other than those of civil and religious liberty—they appeal to the tribunals, and they consider this as worthy and as efficient as the appeal to spiritual weapons, the agitation of conscience, or the resignation of martyrdom.

Can the success of Catholicism be explained by the *voluntary* system, or by causes of a more general order? If we should accept the first explanation—in view of such a striking coincidence—should we also generalize the American example and attribute to this system, in regard to the Catholic Church, a character of excellence as universal as the spirit of that church? This is indeed a serious matter. I will only say that *a priori* and from a theoretical point of view, the application of the *voluntary* system to the Catholic religion offers a system of balanced forces, an intimate alliance of symmetrical principles, and that this conception is very appealing to the mind. The American Catholic Church is a religious society existing at the same time through authority and through liberty, and which applies each of these two principles in the domain in which they belong, the first in divine matters, the second in temporal matters.

The existence of any religion implies that there is only one truth and that the dogma is immutable. The religion does not have the right to impose them on consciences with temporal weapons, but it must affirm them and reject from its bosom the unbelieving or rebel souls. A doctrine not entrusted to a body responsible for its conservation or wavering according to personal interpretations and fantasies cannot constitute a religion. A society of people free, or almost so, to think what they want might well be a civil aggregation, a gathering animated with religious intentions, but it will never be a religious community! The force of Catholicism, apart from the matter of faith, rests undoubtedly in the fixity of its confession (a fixity represented and maintained by the church) organized from bottom up and submitted to a unique supremacy emanating from itself. Well, the American Catholic community obeys this spiritual tutelage, this supremacy. So much for the authority!

It is within the circle of its social existence that this same community places and practices liberty. The clergy move in the midst of the civil society and have no explanations to give other than those which society requires from any citizen. They establish schools, seminaries, all kinds of associations, build churches, tax their members, sell, buy, own, and rule to their liking the temporal and the spiritual matters of their churches with the complete independence characteristic of the system of self-government. So liberty shows its existence!

One can also imagine this clergy as receiving their ministry from the hands of authority and exercising it through those of liberty. It is in this sense that the ecclesiastical organization of

Catholicism, based on the *voluntary* system—as it is practiced in America—seems to me to approach closely the ideal pursued in vain in most human institutions, the conciliation of the two principles which agitated the world from the beginning of societies.

The end of the history of Congregationalism marks the beginning of Unitarianism. . . .

In 1820 Boston was the center of Unitarianism, but it was spread rather uniformly throughout New England. In general, the members were recruited among the higher classes of society; it included the men most commendable for their knowledge, their morality, their philanthropy. The Unitarian pastors were known for their evangelical virtues, their charity, and the elevation of their ideas. The most representative Unitarian is the well-known Channing [William Ellery], one of the men who felt most deeply the love of mankind as the modern mind tends to understand and practice it.

One should not believe, furthermore, that the Unitarians were pleased, at first, by the encroachment of rationalism, under whatever form it appeared (whether it be the ironic, and contemptible Voltairean philosophy, or the learned mystic and theological form of contemporary German philosophy). Though distinguished for their knowledge and education, the leaders of Unitarianism, such as Channing, were not erudite or metaphysicians. Their faith was naive and based on sentiment; they believed in miracles, or at least in most miracles. The Holy Book was the result of a divine inspiration which, if not responsible for each detail, was nevertheless unassailable in regard to the overall meaning of the work. Their first doubt came from their heart, not from their soul. They rejected the Trinity, not because of the metaphysical difficulty for the human reason to admit such mystery, but because they saw in this aspect of the dogma the basis for a pitiless doctrine, destructive of all justice and human brotherhood.

It is only later, after 1830, that Hegelian philosophy crossed the Atlantic. Amid a nation not very open to the novelties of transcendental philosophy, the new philosophy found refuge in the bosom of Unitarianism. It is said that it completely changed its spirit. I do not need to tell you the views of most men who no longer believe in the supernatural or the letter of any revelation—though still feeling the spur of the religious spirit and of a divine curiosity no longer satisfied. They consider all religions, from the most primitive fetishism to the most refined Christianism, as developments of the divine idea, an idea inherent in mankind and forming the thread of all the intellectual and moral accomplishments of men since the beginning of time. Among all the revealers who appeared on the world stage and who personified to various degrees the mystery of the absolute union of God and man, or rather the mystery of divine nature manifesting itself in human nature, none had, as much as Jesus Christ, the sentiment and the intimate consciousness of the celestial origin of man. It is in this sense that He was truly the Son of God.

I suppose that if we should examine the present doctrines of the Unitarians, one would find something of the transcendental philosophy. Each one must decide whether this is still Christianism, and if it is possible to find in these philosophical conceptions the elements of any religion. Of course, American Protestant churches refuse the brotherly title of evangelical church—a general name which includes them all, Episcopal, Presbyterian, Methodist, Baptist, etc.—to Unitarianism. In their classification, they place the Roman Catholics beside the Unitarians—as non-evangelical churches—apologizing to the former for placing their name next to that of an anti-Christian church.

Hatreds are very strong. American Protestantism is aware of the dangers which threaten it. Rationalism when it is coarsely impious, philosophical, or learned is not to be feared in the United States. But under the disguise of Unitarianism it presents a real danger. The American needs a religion, a temple, a minister. His relationships with his church, though not marked with a very exalted mysticism, constitute the only aspect of his life touching the ideal. He does not have any others, absorbed as he is with his work, his practical occupations, and his very concrete mental

activity. If he should withdraw the Idea of God from his existence, he would be powerless to fill, or even conceal, the huge
gap in his soul with the more or less spiritual speculations of
philosophy which may, up to a certain point, deceive consciences
and amuse them. For fear of being delivered defenseless to the
devouring enemy, absolute positivism, he needs a cult, a predic-
tion. In a word, he must occasionally open his window to the
heavens in order to breathe. Furthermore, the administrative
occupations he imposes upon himself—because of his church—
are quite to his liking and amuse him infinitely. To meet with
people of the same class, that is to say, the same fortune; to
organize an assembly, to vote funds, to ask for treasurers' reports,
to compete in luxury and comfort with the neighboring church—
to rob it, if possible, of its renowned preacher—finally to practice
free association for any goal whatsoever, these are for the
Americans very keen pleasures and distractions that nothing in
their monotonous existence could ever replace.

Well, Unitarianism offers all of that to them! Whatever its
dogma might be, it scrupulously conserved the cult and sacraments of Calvinism, baptism, the Lord's Supper, and the whole
ecclesiastical organization of Congregationalism. Today no sect
has better built, more comfortable, and better kept temples. No
other religion can boast more respected and more respectable,
more eloquent and more practical ministers. Finally, the new
sect counts among its members the first citizens of the United
States, the men distinguished among all others by their position,
knowledge, public and private virtues.

This is why Unitarianism is the most formidable of the enemies
which Protestantism must fight. Purposefully, I do not mention
Catholicism, for I believe it is not directly threatened. I do not
mean that the very essence of Christian religion—and for that
matter of any revealed religion—is not attacked by a school that
does not believe in the supernatural! Still, for the moment,
Protestantism is directly challenged. Through Unitarianism, modern skepticism entered the very heart of the weakest and most
vulnerable of the two great Christian faiths. Catholicism has a

great advantage: its enemies might fight it, but they cannot enter its bosom! Catholicism is inexorable; it always severs pitilessly any part of the church which may seem gangrenous. The danger can only come from the outside. Unlike the Episcopal, the German Lutheran, and the American Congregationalist churches, Catholicism will never be torn from within, or poisoned at the very source of its life by its own ministers. Any doubtful Catholic priest immediately ceases to be a Catholic priest. The same cannot be said of the Christian sects created by the Reformation. Protestantism, throughout all of its religious development, professed at one time or another the complete series of theological doctrines which it is possible for man to bring to light. The true spirit of Protestantism refuses to draw a clear line between truth and error; it refuses to accept one and reject the other. Its altars are open to all—the most childish faith as well as the most unmanageable skepticism. When attacked, Catholicism tightens its discipline, reinforces its doctrines, and refuses any concession. Above all, and unlike Protestantism, it is careful not to assert yesterday's miracles by denying today's. It imposes contemporary miracles upon the faithful, aware that he who is allowed to introduce chronological distinctions into the supernatural is close to losing his belief in it.

Protestantism, thus, is an easy prey for rationalism. The latter feeds on the very substance of Protestantism. It takes away its name, its ministers, and temples, until, someday, this great body, gradually deteriorating within a still living shell, will be nothing but a useless skeleton which will disappear into dust. Rationalism, then, will be face to face with Catholicism, as the latter alone will have survived the disappearance of all other religious sects. The fight between these two champions will decide the future destinies of mankind.

SOURCES

The following information has reference to editions of works from which excerpts were taken—not necessarily the first editions.

1. WHITEFIELD, GEORGE, *A Continuation of the Reverend Mr. White-field's Journal, from His Embarking after the Embargo to His Arrival at Savannah in Georgia* (Second edition, London: James Hutton, 1740), pp. 34–5, 36–7, 40–2, 43–5, 48, 49.
   ——, *A Continuation of the Reverend Mr. Whitefield's Journal, from a Few Days after His Return to Georgia to His Arrival at Falmouth, on the 11th of March 1741* . . . (London: R. Hett, 1741), pp. 15–16, 24–5, 54–5.

2. HAMILTON, ALEXANDER, *Gentleman's Progress: The Itinerarium of Dr. Alexander Hamilton*, edited by Carl Bridenbaugh (Chapel Hill: University of North Carolina Press, 1948), pp. 10, 20, 22–3, 31–3, 34–5, 57–9, 119–20.

3. KALM, PETER, *Travels into North America*, translated by John Reinhold Forster (London: for the editor, 1770–1771), pp. 36–43, 25–9.

4. CRÈVECOEUR, MICHEL-GUILLAUME JEAN DE, *Letters from an American Farmer* (New York: Fox, Duffield and Company, 1904), pp. 54–8, 61–6.

5. COKE, THOMAS, *The Life of the Rev. John Wesley, A. M.; Including an Account of the Great Revival of Religion in Europe and America, of Which He Was the First and Chief Instrument* (first American edition, Philadelphia: John Dickins, 1793), pp. 341–2, 343–5, 350–3.

6. COBBETT, WILLIAM, *Journal of a Year's Residence in the United States of America* . . . , in three parts (London: Sherwood, Neely and Jones, 1819), Part II, pp. 406, 413, 418–21, 423–7.

7. MURAT, ACHILLE, *A Moral and Political Sketch of the United States of North America* (London: Effingham Wilson, 1833), pp. 111–6, 117–8, 132–6, 142–4.

8. LEVASSEUR, AUGUSTE, *Lafayette in America in 1824 and 1825, or, Journal of a Voyage to the United States . . .* , two volumes, translated by John D. Godman (Philadelphia: Carey and Lea, 1829), Vol. I, pp. 28, 57, 172–4, 222–4; Vol. II, pp. 260–1.

9. TROLLOPE, FRANCES, *The Domestic Manners of the Americans*, two volumes (New York: Dodd, Mead and Company, 1901), Vol. I, pp. 101–4, 149–55; Vol. II, pp. 224–5.

10. GRUND, FRANCIS, *The Americans in Their Moral, Social, and Political Relations*, two volumes (London: Longman, Green, et. al., 1837), Vol. I, pp. 56–64, 255–6, 291–6, 301–3.

11. TOCQUEVILLE, ALEXIS DE, *Democracy in America*, trans. Henry Reeve (Boston: John Allyn, 1876), Volume One, pp. 387–402.

12. REED, ANDREW (with James Matheson), *Narrative of the Visit to the American Churches, by the Deputation from the Congregational Union of England and Wales*, two volumes (New York: Harper and Brothers, 1835), Vol. II, pp. 91, 93–8, 98–100, 101–8, 194, 197.

13. MARTINEAU, HARRIET, *Society in America*, two volumes (New York: Saunders and Otley, 1837), Vol. II, pp. 314–8, 337–40, 348–66.

14. COMBE, GEORGE, *Notes on the United States of North America, during a Phrenological Visit in 1838–9–40*, two volumes (Edinburgh: MacLachlan, Stewart, and Company, 1841), Vol. I, pp. 98–9, 132–9; Vol. II, pp. 210–2, 250, 286.

15. SCHAFF, PHILIP, *America: A Sketch of Its Political, Social, and Religious Character*, translated by Edward D. Yeomans, edited by Perry Miller (Cambridge: The Belknap Press, 1961), pp. 72–81, 96–104.

16. GODLEY, JOHN ROBERT, *Letters From America*, two volumes (London: John Murray, 1844), Vol. II, pp. 104–6, 124–32, 224–8, 237–9.

17. DIXON, JAMES, *Methodism in America* (London: for the author, 1849), pp. 138–9, 140–9.

18. FERRI-PISANI, CAMILLE, *Prince Napoleon in America, 1861*, translated by George J. Joyaux (Bloomington: Indiana University Press, 1959), pp. 278, 288–98, 301–6. Reprinted by permission.

SUGGESTIONS FOR
FURTHER READING

Students of American religion have at their disposal what is perhaps the best bibliography on a specific aspect of American life in Nelson Burr, *A Critical Bibliography of Religion in America* (Princeton: Princeton University Press, 1957). For travel literature, Frank Monaghan, *French Travellers in the United States, 1765–1932: A Bibliography* (New York: New York Public Library, 1933), and Thomas D. Clark, *Travels in the Old South: A Bibliography* (Norman: University of Oklahoma Press, 1956–1959) are particularly helpful.

Two recent surveys of religion in America are especially recommended: Clifton E. Olmstead, *History of Religion in the United States* (Englewood Cliffs, N. J.: Prentice-Hall, 1960), and Winthrop S. Hudson, *Religion in America* (New York: Charles Scribner's Sons, 1965).

Winthrop S. Hudson, *The Great Tradition of the American Churches* (New York: Harper, 1953) stresses the centrality of the voluntary principle in American Protestantism. An excellent, brief interpretation, available in paperback is Franklin H. Littell, *From State Church to Pluralism* (Garden City, N. Y.: Doubleday, 1962).

H. Richard Niebuhr's pioneering study *The Social Sources of Denominationalism* (New York: Henry Holt, 1929) is essential to any adequate understanding of the voluntary church. Sidney Mead, *The Lively Experiment* (New York: Harper & Row, 1963) is the best study of the origins and development of the voluntary system in America.

Jerald C. Brauer discusses the insights into American church history provided by several nineteenth-century visitors, especially de Tocqueville, in "Images of Religion in America," *Church History*, Vol. XXX,

No. 1 (March 1961), pp. 3–18. Travelers' comments on a wide variety of topics other than religion can be found in three collections: Allan Nevins (ed.), *America Through British Eyes* (revised edition, New York: Oxford University Press, 1948), Henry Steele Commager (ed.), *America in Perspective: The United States Through Foreign Eyes* (New York: Random House, 1947), and Oscar Handlin (ed.), *This Was America* (Cambridge: Harvard University Press, 1949). Anson Phelps Stokes, *Church and State in the United States* (New York: Harper & Bros., 1950), Three Volumes, is both a comprehensive survey of the subject and a valuable guide to the sources.